SADHU SUNDAR SINGH

SADHU SUNDAR SINGH

Phyllis Thompson

OM Publishing
Carlisle

Scripture quotations are taken from the New
International Version, © 1973, 1978, 1984 by International
Bible Society and published in Britain by Hodder and
Stoughton Ltd.

British Library Cataloguing-in-Publication Data.
A catalogue record for this book
is available from the British Library.

ISBN 1-85078-099-4

OM Publishing is an imprint of
Send The Light (Operation Mobilisation),
PO Box 300, Carlisle, Cumbria, CA3 0QS, UK

Production and printing in England by
Nuprint Ltd, Station Road, Harpenden, Herts AL5 4SE.

AUTHOR'S PREFACE

Over a century ago, on 3 September 1889, a Sikh
mother gave birth to her youngest son in a remote
village in the Punjab. He was born into the family of a
landowner, wealthy enough by local standards, but of
little importance in an India ruled by the British Raj.
Those were the days when Indians were second-class
citizens in their own country, when they could be
ejected unprotesting from a railway carriage into
which a European wished to deposit himself and his
luggage. Hindus, Muslims and Sikhs alike had to
accept the supremacy of the white man who was
almost like a being from another world, a caste to
himself, living apart from the masses of the land he
had temporarily conquered. Yet from among those
masses in an out of the way Punjab village emerged a
figure whose short life of less than forty years influenced not only multitudes in his own country, but
also in the western world.

I had heard about Sadhu Sundar Singh, of course,
and had read one or two books about him, but not
until Send The Light asked me to write a fresh biogra-

phy did I settle down to make a study of the life of this Indian Christian mystic. I am indebted to Dave Brown for all the help he has given, not least in providing me with several of the books listed below, as the basis for research. I must also thank the Evangelical Library for the long loan of *Sundar Singh: A Biography* by A. J. Appasamy.

I am very conscious of the shortcomings of what I have written, but as Sundar Singh himself wrote,

'There is nothing so perfect in the world as to be quite above objection and criticism. The very sun which gives us light and warmth is not free from spots, yet notwithstanding these defects it does not desist from its regular duty. It behoves us in like manner to carry on to the best of our ability what has been entrusted to us...'

Phyllis Thompson

ACKNOWLEDGEMENTS

I am deeply indebted to the authors and publishers of the following books and magazines:

Life in Abundance (Sermons of the Sadhu), Edited by A. F. Thyagaraju, The Christian Literature Society (India)

Sadhu Sundar Singh: Called of God, Rebecca Parker, The Christian Literature Society (India)

The Vision and The Call, T. E. Riddle, Indian Society for Promoting Christian Knowledge

Sundar Singh: A Biography, A. J. Appasamy, Lutterworth Press

The Sadhu, Streeter and Appasamy, McMillan and Co. Ltd.

Sadhu Sundar Singh, Cyril J. Davey, STL Books

The Saffron Robe, Janet Lynch-Watson, Hodder and Stoughton

The Christian Witness of Sadhu Sundar Singh, T. Dayanandan Francis (Ed.), The Christian Literature Society (India)

Sadhu Sundar Singh: He Walked with God, Joshua Daniel, Layman's Evangelical Fellowship

Sundar Singh: Lion-hearted Warrior, E. Sanders and Ethelred Judah, Society for Promoting Christian Knowledge (London)

Sadhu Sundar Singh: The Lover of the Cross, T. Dayanandan Francis, The Christian Literature Society (India)

Another Daniel, Joshua Daniel, Layman's Evangelical Fellowship

Monsoon Daybreak, R. R. Rajamani, Open Books

Books by Sadhu Sundar Singh, published by The Christian Literature Society, Madras, India:

> *At the Master's Feet*
> *Reality and Religion*
> *The Real Life*
> *The Spiritual World*
> *The Spiritual Life*
> *The Search after Reality*
> *With and Without Christ*

Magazines:
The Family Magazine of the Diocese of Madras, June 1989
The North India Churchman, Meadows, September 1989

'Sundar Singh's personality might be described as primitive and evangelical, with however, a tendency towards pietistic subjectivity and a non-ecclesiastical individualism. He represents a simple, childlike, and yet clear and spiritual religious faith, based entirely upon the New Testament.'

Friedrich Heiler

THE FUTURE LIFE

Belief in the future life has been found among all nations at all times. Desires imply a possible fulfilment. Thirst implies the existence of water, and hunger of food. The desire to live for ever is itself a proof of its fulfilment.

Again, we have some higher, nobler desires of the Spirit which cannot be fulfilled in this world. Therefore there must be another spiritual world in which those desires can be met. This material world cannot by any means satisfy our spiritual cravings.

The soul's real desire can only be satisfied by God who has created the soul and the desire for him inherent in it. Because God has created man in his own likeness, man has in him something of the divine nature which longs for fellowship with him. Like seeks like by the laws of being. And when we are rooted in the Eternal Being, we shall not only feel satisfied, but also have eternal life in him.

Reality and Religion

1

The Ludhiana express was thundering across the Punjab plain, and although he could not yet hear it, young Sundar Singh, crouching in his room, knew it would pass along the track bordering his father's estate in half an hour's time. There was no doubt about that. The train was always punctual, and very soon now he would put his plan into action. Time was running out. He had decided that if the unknown God to whom he had been praying so desperately did not reveal himself before five o'clock that morning, he would fling himself on the line for the train to pass over him. He could bear the turmoil in his heart and mind no longer.

At fifteen years of age he was prepared to commit suicide. And strangely enough, it was the mother whom he had loved so ardently, and who had so loved him, who had been largely responsible for bringing about this state of mind.

His mother had always been known in her family and the community in which she lived, as a deeply religious woman. Certainly her little son knew her to be so. At a very early age he was made aware of it. When he woke each morning he saw his mother, already bathed and dressed, poring over the *Bhagavad Gita* and other Hindu scriptures. He knew she was seeking Something or Someone she could not see, and this consciousness of the unseen was early impressed on him. She insisted, as soon as he was old enough to understand, that he must follow the same pattern — he must be bathed, then learn something from the holy books before he had his breakfast. So deeply was the habit ingrained in him that although, when very small, he sometimes demanded unsuccessfully that he must have his breakfast first, it soon became his second nature to rise, bathe, then apply his mind to the books before giving a thought to food.

Throughout those early years, when he grew from babyhood to childhood, his mother was the dominating influence of his life. She was always there. And she was always conscious of him. He knew that. He would see her in the kitchen, superintending the cooking, doing much of it herself, while the servants busied themselves cleaning, fetching and carrying — but from time to time her gaze would dart in his direction, and a little smile come over her face when she caught his eye. When she sat, the big brass tray of food in front of her, and the other members of the family sitting around, she was never too preoccupied to notice when he opened his mouth and immediately pop into it a little piece of chappati dipped in one of his favourite spices. She knew which flavours he liked best, and although he did not always get exactly what he wanted, she explained patiently that what she was giving him was good for him, and would make him grow strong like his brothers. When he toddled to her with something he had discovered, or wanted her to look at, she would put aside what she

12

was doing, and give him her attention. And he always knew where to go when he was hurt, sobbing out his short-lived grief on her bosom. His mother was the centre to which he instinctively gravitated, and from which he was never turned away.

She bathed him, rubbed him in oil, washed his thickly growing hair, clothed him, fed him, and took him with her to the Hindu temples where she went to worship. Although a Sikh, she did not believe that spiritual truth was only to be found in the religion of the Sikhs. In fact, the book to which she introduced him, acting as his first teacher, was the Hindu *Bhagavad Gita*, and by the time he was seven he knew it by heart. It was one of the highlights of his young life to be taken by her across the dusty plain to the jungle in which an old *sadhu* lived, to be tested in his knowledge and understanding of it. The old *sadhu* lived alone in the jungle, withdrawn from the world of men in order that he could the better seek the Unseen. There was a calmness about him, and a dignity that was slightly awesome, and yet appealing. Sundar was not afraid as the old man looked down on him and started asking him questions, and he answered clearly and confidently.

'Tell me, Sundar, how can we please God?'

'By obeying the Laws our fathers have taught us,' Sundar replied.

'Good! Is there any other way to please God?'

'We please God when we think about him. We please God if we do not want to be rich, if we do not want to have a lot of money. We please God when we are poor, and live alone, far from other people. We please God when we try to find peace, like the *sadhus*.'

So the examination went on, the old *sadhu* nodding approvingly. 'The boy answers well,' he told

13

Sundar's mother. 'Perhaps one day he will become a *sadhu*.' Nothing could have pleased her better. This would be the height of her ambition for her son, and Sundar realised it. He was too young to think much about becoming a *sadhu*, but he was not too young to begin to wonder what it was that his mother, and the religious people to whom she went, were seeking.

His mother explained, as best she could, what it was. There was a peace of heart, a peace in one's innermost being, that could only be obtained by earnest seeking, and it was the greatest treasure anyone could possess. Worldly success, earthly enjoyment, the possession of wealth and power, all the variety of gratifying experiences that people according to their temperaments sought for, were not to be compared with it. This peace of heart was spiritual, and it was completely satisfying, but it was very difficult to obtain. She wanted it herself, but even more, perhaps, she wanted her little son to have it.

'You must not do anything wrong,' she told him. 'This is very important. And what is more, you must be kind to other people, especially to people in trouble.' He saw that she always gave food to beggars, and to the 'holy men' who wandered from village to village, the *sadhus* and *sanyasis* who had renounced their homes and their families, their money, everything in order to seek peace, and deliverance from the wheel of life with its endless reincarnations. The *sadhus* had chosen that path early in life, while the *sanyasis* had done so much later, often when already entangled with the claims of family and property — and perhaps of debt.

Whatever may have been the background from which they came, they had now taken the path of renunciation, and Sundar's mother respected them for it. It was an act of merit to provide them with food and shelter as they passed on their pilgrimage from one shrine to another, however dirty and unkempt they were. They who renounced the world were more to be venerated than they who ruled it.

Not that Sundar's mother could not discern differences even between the 'holy men'. She was a sincere and intelligent woman, and since she was determined that her youngest son should have all the spiritual help possible, she made her choice of teachers for him very carefully. She put him to study under a Hindu teacher and a Sikh *sadhu*, and they both found their young pupil disconcertingly earnest in his desire to discover for himself the peace they talked about and read to him about. How was it obtained?

He asked them questions that perplexed them, and he would not accept their explanations that it took a very long time, and that as he increased in knowledge the problems that he had in his mind about it would gradually disappear. He *was* increasing in knowledge as he studied under them, he argued, but instead of disappearing, the knowledge he gained only made him more worried. They explained that as he grew older and more experienced in spiritual things, he would understand.

'But suppose I don't grow up?' he insisted. 'Suppose I die when I am still young, and have not got it.'

The answer to that one was easier. 'If you die when you are young, then you will get this peace in your next rebirth, if you keep on trying for it. And if not the next, then the one after, or the one after that — if you keep on trying...! And now, you are too young to worry about these things. Go along and play,' they told him, and his father said the same. It wasn't natural for a boy of his age to be worrying about these things. He ought to be out with his older brothers,

15

joining in their games. And he ought not to stay up so late, reading. It was bad for his health.

'I expect you get it from your mother,' he said with a shrug. He was a good Sikh, and respected his wife, even approved her religious tendencies up to a point, although he felt she went too far when it came to impressing them on young Sundar. Yet he freely expressed his intense gratification at his youngest son's behaviour in the matter of the stolen five rupees.

This incident was one that was forever engraved on Sundar's memory. It started on the day his father gave him a few coins to spend as he liked, and he ran off happily to the bazaar to see what he could find. On the way there he saw an old low-caste woman, huddled up by the wayside. She wore only a few thin rags, and as Sundar approached her she automatically gave a pitiful whine and held out a thin, claw-like hand, begging. It was no unusual sight to him, but this time Sundar's heart was touched. The weather was cold, and he was reminded of his mother's insistence about being kind to people in need. Instead of going on to the bazaar to spend his money, he impulsively gave it all to the old woman, then ran home to find his father.

'There's an old woman begging in the road,' he said breathlessly. 'And she hasn't got enough clothes. She's shivering, and she hasn't got a blanket. Please give her money to buy a blanket.'

'Oh, I know that old woman,' his father replied. 'I've helped her several times in the past. Now it's someone else's turn to do something.'

'But suppose no one does help her! Suppose she dies of cold!' His pleas were in vain, his father refused to listen to him, and walked away. Disappointed, Sundar turned away too, but he could not forget the old woman, and the desire to help her grew into a determination to do so. Then he saw a coat of his father's

16

lying on a bench, and looking quickly round to make sure he was alone, he slipped his hand into one of the pockets and drew out some coins. Five rupees! Enough to buy the old woman a blanket, he thought, and although it was too late to do anything that day, he decided he would take the money, and give it to her the next morning. He hoped his father would not notice the loss of the coins.

But his father was more aware of how much money he had in his pocket than Sundar realised. Sometime later his father came in, picked up the coat, and searching in his pocket drew out the few coins left there and said with a puzzled frown,

'I had more than this...' Then he looked at Sundar and asked,

'Have you taken any money from my pocket?'

'No,' said Sundar promptly, and to his relief his father said no more.

His relief lasted only a very short time. If he had never been conscious of it before Sundar realised now, with acute discomfort, that he had a conscience. He went to bed that night feeling very unhappy — far too unhappy to sleep. On the one hand he argued with himself that he had been right in wanting to help the old woman, but on the other hand his conscience told him he had been wrong to steal the money, especially from his own father. And then to lie deliberately to cover up his theft!

Long before the night was over Sundar knew what he must do. However painful the consequences, he had to tell his father what he had done, and return the money. Anything would be better than to go on living with his accusing conscience. Very early in the morning he got up, went out into the courtyard to bathe and wash his hair, as usual, then he went to his father's room, the five rupees in his hand, to tell the whole story.

It is not surprising that this incident was one of the outstanding experiences of his childhood, for it turned out entirely differently to what he expected and feared.

It is doubtful whether either Sundar or his father had ever heard the immortal story known as 'The Prodigal Son', but what happened between them that day bore out its universal character, and insight into a father's heart. Certainly it was an experience that Sundar himself never forgot.

Exactly what he said to his father he did not remember, except that everything came out — the desire to help the old woman, the theft, then the lie, followed by a sleepless night and the realisation that he must return the money — not secretly, but by making a full confession. What he never forgot was his father's reaction as he stood there, manfully telling the whole shameful story. Instead of the expression of anger he had expected, and the harsh upbraiding, followed perhaps by a thrashing, he saw tears come into his father's eyes, saw him hold out his arms and heard him say with a little choke in his voice,

'My son!' Then, feeling himself hugged, feeling his father's hand stroking his head, he heard the words,

'My son! I always knew I could trust you. And now I know I was not wrong!'

His father still trusted him! All his remorse and shame and fear were submerged in a flood of relief and gratitude, as he realised that he was completely reinstated. It was as though he had never stolen the money, never told a lie to cover it up. That dark incident was not only forgiven — it was forgotten.

Nothing more was said about it, but as his father turned away to go off to his business, he said,

'I'll buy a blanket for that old woman with these five rupees.' Then he added with a smile, drawing a coin out of his pocket and handing it to Sundar,

'Here's a rupee for yourself — go and buy some sweets with it!'

Although Sundar's mother was largely responsible for his spiritual instruction, his father saw to it that he had the best secular education available to him. A small primary school had been opened by an American Presbyterian Mission in the village, and Sundar was enrolled as one of the pupils. Christians generally were regarded with contempt by Sikhs, Muslims and Hindus alike, but if the missionaries from the west were prepared to supply their children with a good education, they saw no reason for not taking advantage of it. Sundar's father took a tolerant view of other religions, and the fact that the Bible was included as one of the subjects in the school curriculum did not worry him.

Sundar himself, however, strongly resented it. He was a Sikh. The *Granth* was the Sikh's holy book, and had been since the Tenth Guru, when asked as he was dying whom he would name as his successor, had placed his hand on it and said, 'This is your Guru.' The *Granth* commanded as deep a reverence from the Sikh as the idol in the temple from the Hindu. But the Hindus had their holy books too, such as the *Bhagavad Gita*. Sundar was constantly studying them, since his mother and the *sadhus* assured him that in their teachings he would find the peace he was already longing to obtain. But this book of the despised Christians — why should he, a Sikh, be compelled to read it, hear it explained, answer questions about its contents day after day?

He was a rebel. As much as he dared he made a

nuisance of himself in class by interrupting the Bible lessons with awkward remarks and questions. For some reason which he himself would have found it difficult to explain, he really hated Christianity and everything connected with it. And when Christian evangelists turned up to preach openly in the bazaar, Sundar was the ring leader of a little group of boys who pelted them with stones before scampering off to avoid trouble. Neither of his parents knew about this, for it is certain that neither of them would have approved. Such violence was contrary to the nature and spiritual principles of his mother, while his father, though proud enough of being a Sikh, preserved a 'live and let live' attitude towards followers of other religions.

But Sundar, it seemed, always went to extremes. On the one hand he hated Christianity violently. On the other hand, he started to practise yoga, mastering to some extent the technique by which he became oblivious of external things, sitting immobile that he might meditate, and even attaining, for brief spells, the peace of soul for which he yearned. The brief spells did not last long, and back he would be in as uneasy and discontented a state as before.

The great tragedy of his life occurred when he was about fourteen. His mother died.

What her loss meant to him no one else knew. She had been the one to whom he could always turn, the one who sensed intuitively what he was feeling, the one who touched deeper chords in his spirit than any other. And now she was gone. The big courtyards around which the flat-roofed houses of the Singhs were built were alive with other members of the family, but he knew it was useless for his eyes to glance quickly around to find her. She was not there, and never would be again. She was lost forever, as far as

20

he or anyone else who had known her was concerned. Even if she were there re-born in another form, he would not know her.

The *sadhus* and the teachers had no comfort for him. It was the same when his elder brother, the one to whom he was specially attached, died a few months later. He, too, had been carried away on the wheel of life, to be reincarnated in another unrecognisable form, and Sundar must bow to his fate in the loss of these two whom he had loved. They were taken from him, as sooner or later they must be, anyway. The fact that it was so early in his life was his fate. It was the law of *Karma*, the inevitability of fate, and nothing could alter it. He must accept it.

All the more reason to seek for union with the Supreme Spirit, since there only can be found a peace that delivers from all feelings, either of grief or joy. Sundar continued such a search, but without the inspiration of his mother's presence and example, it was more difficult.

Meanwhile, human nature that unconsciously demanded an outlet, had to hit out against something. His animosity against Christianity had lain dormant for a time because with the opening of a Government school three miles away he had been sent there, where nothing was taught to arouse his resentment. But the long daily walk to and from school in the hot weather proved too much for him, and he was transferred back to the Mission school in Rampur. Again he was compelled to study the Bible, and although, against his will, he found himself attracted by some of the things he read, he was still convinced that it was false, and determined to oppose it.

He opposed it, eventually, in quite a dramatic manner. Obtaining possession of one of the Gospels one day, and calling some of his school friends to see what

21

he would do with it, he tore it in half, then set light to it.

'That's what I think of it!' he said defiantly. But his father, seeing what he had done, scolded him. It was the holy book of the Christians, and ought not to be treated in that way, he said. If Sundar did not want it, he ought to have returned it to the missionary.

It was only a few days after this incident that Sundar came to the point of desperation that led him to the decision to throw himself under the Ludhiana express if God did not reveal to him the true way of peace. Find that way he must, either in this world or the next. He had made up his mind.

At three o'clock in the morning he rose from his bed and went out into the moonlit courtyard for the ceremonial bathe observed by devout Hindus and Sikhs before worship. Then he returned to his room and knelt down, bowing his head to the ground, pleading that God would reveal himself. He prayed, then waited silent and expectant, then prayed again.

But nothing happened. He had not known what to expect, whether he would hear a voice, see a vision, go into a trance... But nothing happened. And time was passing. In half an hour the Ludhiana express would come thundering along the line...

He lifted his head and opened his eyes, and was rather surprised to see a faint cloud of light in the room. It was too early for the dawn, and thinking it might have come from the courtyard, he opened the door and peered out. All was in darkness. Turning back into the room, he saw that the light in the room was getting brighter. Then, to his amazement, in it he saw the radiant figure and face, not of Buddha, nor of Krishna, but of Jesus Christ.

Jesus Christ was there in the room, shining, radiating joy and peace and love, looking at him with compassion, and asking,

'Why do you persecute me? I died for you...'

PERFECTION

According to the laws of Nature, it is necessary to grow gradually by stages in order to attain perfection. In this way alone can we make ourselves ready and fit for the destiny for which we have been created. Sudden or hurried progress leaves us weak and imperfect. The oats which grow in a few weeks in Lapland do not yield the same nourishment as the wheat which takes six months to ripen. The bamboo grows three feet daily and shoots up one hundred and eighty-five feet, but it remains empty and hollow within. Slow and gradual progress, therefore, is necessary for perfection.

It is true that perfection can be attained only in a perfect environment. But before entering the perfect environment we have to pass through an imperfect environment, where we have to make effort and struggle. This struggle makes us strong and ready for the perfect environment, just as the silkworm's struggle in the cocoon enables it to emerge as a beautiful butterfly. When we reach the perfect state, we shall see how these things which seem to have hindered us have really helped us, though mysteriously, to reach perfection.

In man, there are seeds of countless qualities which cannot develop in this world because the means here are not conducive towards their growth and development towards perfection. In the world to come they will find the environment necessary for the attainment of perfection. But the growth must begin here.

Reality and Religion

Chapter

2

The revelation of God to the human soul is granted in innumerable ways, different in every case. As each human soul has its distinctive features, so God's dealings with each varies according to need, and according to his own inscrutable purpose. Yet in many cases there are similarities. Sundar's experience on that memorable night is reminiscent of what happened to Saul of Tarsus on the road to Damascus eighteen hundred years before. Sundar, like Saul, had been bitterly opposed to believers in Christ. Like Saul he was arrested by the divine appearance of the glorified Christ himself. Like Saul, the first words he heard were in the form of a question:

'Why do you persecute me?'

Like Saul that interview, brief as it was as we count time, marked the turning point in his life. Years later he described what happened.

'I remained till about half past four praying and waiting and expecting to see Krishna or Buddha, or some other *Avatar* of the Hindu religion; they appeared not, but a light was shining in the room. I opened the door to see where it came from, but all was dark outside. I returned inside, and the light increased in intensity and took the form of a globe of light above the ground, and in this light there appeared, not the form I expected, but the living Christ whom I had counted as dead. To all eternity I shall never forget his glorious and loving face, nor the few words which he spoke.

' "Why do you persecute me? See, I have died on the cross for you and for the whole world." These words were burned into my heart as by lightning, and I fell on the ground before him. My heart was filled with inexpressible joy and peace, and my whole life was entirely changed.'

The Ludhiana express roared along the line until the sound of it was lost in the distance, but Sundar had not even heard it. As he bowed to the ground, alone in his room, the Sikh schoolboy was submerged in a flood of relief and with an inexpressible sense of well being. All the bewilderment and anger, frustration and despair that had been increasing over the past months were swallowed up in a moment, forgotten in the splendour and reality of that utterly unexpected revelation. His young heart went out in adoration to the One who had shown himself so convincingly and so lovingly. He made no conscious commitment, probably did not even think of his own future.

He was still a young teenager, with all the enthusiasm and impetuosity of youth. The amazing experience had to be shared, and his new allegiance made known. Before dawn, while the courtyard was still empty, he slipped into his father's room and woke him up.

'I have seen Jesus Christ! He appeared to me in my room just now. I have become a Christian…'

Not surprisingly, his father was unfavourably impressed, and said so.

'What are you talking about, you silly boy! Only three days ago you burned the Christians' book, and now you say you are a Christian yourself! Go back to bed. I want to go to sleep.' He turned over and closed his eyes. As far as he was concerned, that was the end of the matter. Or so he thought. But he soon discovered it was not the end of the matter for Sundar. His youngest son was talking to other members of the family, talking about this vision he had seen, and although they all reacted in the same way, telling Sundar he had imagined it, or had had a bad dream, or that he was going mad, Sundar never had a doubt as to what he had seen and heard.

It so happened that one of his school friends was the son of the headmaster, and to this boy Sundar expressed his desire to know how to become a Christian. The boy told his father, and the headmaster found himself in a quandary. It was one thing to have the sons of prominent Sikhs and Hindus in the school, and for it to be understood that the curriculum would include stories from the Bible, and even teaching about the rudiments of Christianity, delivered in an impersonal way. It would be quite another thing to encourage any of them to become Christians.

The tiny Christian minority was drawn mainly from the despised outcastes. Although they were tolerated, largely because the British Raj granted them equal right by law, and because western missionaries improved their living conditions and often supplied them with well-paid jobs, they were still regarded with contempt. The headmaster knew that if any of his pupils of other faiths gave the slightest evidence of turning to Christianity, it would bring down the indignation of the parents, not only on himself, but on the school authorities, and who could tell what that would lead to? Sher Singh, Sundar's father, was an influential man in the neighbourhood, and opposition from him could have a very damaging effect on the Mission as well as the school.

Yet here was this lad, eager to find out all about the religion he had previously derided, asserting that he wanted to be a Christian. How could such fervour be ignored? The headmaster did the best he could in the circumstances. He undertook to teach Sundar the Bible, but to do it secretly. For several months the tuition was conducted out of school hours, and as Sundar read the Scriptures, the Gospels in particular, his heart was increasingly drawn towards the One who had so wonderfully appeared to him on that dark December morning. Tears came to his eyes time and time again as he pondered the quiet majesty of the Man of Galilee whose pathway of suffering led eventually to the cross on Calvary. And his terms of discipleship were imprinted deeply on the mind of the Sikh schoolboy.

'If anyone would come after me, he must deny himself and take up his cross and follow me. For whoever wants to save his life will lose it, but whoever loses his life for me and for the gospel will save it.' (Mark 8:34,35)

He began very early to learn what discipleship would cost him. So did Sirdar, a classmate of his, who had also given expression to his conviction that what the Bible revealed about Jesus Christ was true. The two boys, both from Sikh families, remained firm regarding their faith, in spite of the jibing and even ill treatment they received in their homes when their families realised they were in earnest. For Sundar the ill treatment, principally at the hands of his eldest brother, was easier to endure than the entreaties of his father.

'Don't bring disgrace on your family by joining those dirty outcastes,' he pleaded. The local Christians were mainly of the sweeper caste, and as such did all the dirty work in the village. By the high standards of cleanliness of the Sikhs, they were filthy in their personal habits, and altogether in a vastly inferior social category to the Singhs. In fact, they had no status at all. And to come to the all important matter of their religion, it was contrary to the beliefs of the Sikhs and the Hindus, contrary to the beliefs of Sundar's own family — contrary to the beliefs of his mother. How could he put his family to shame by joining them?

These arguments, for Sundar, were harder to resist than the temptation his uncle placed before him. This honoured elderly member of the family was very wealthy, and one day came and took Sundar to his large, luxurious home. Leading the boy down into a deep cellar, he locked the door behind them both, then went over to a big safe which he opened, telling Sundar to look inside and see what was there. The iron box was filled, not only with money, but with precious jewels as well. The earthly wealth stored there was beyond anything Sundar had ever seen. Then, to his embarrassment, his old uncle promised he should have all of it, if only he would remain a Sikh. He went even farther. Taking off his turban he laid it on Sundar's feet. It was the humblest act of supplication he could make, and Sundar was deeply touched. That the senior member of the Singh family should go to such lengths to keep him, the youngest of them, revealed to him the depth of the anxiety they all felt. It was an evidence of the love they had for him, and he began to experience the cost of discipleship that lay behind the words,

'Anyone who loves his father or mother more than me is not worthy of me…' The claims of family love and loyalty are very strong, and to turn away from them makes demands that cut to the core of the heart. His father's chagrin and disappointment were particularly hard to bear, as well as the increasing ostracism of the rest of the family.

Then things came to a head. The father of his friend, Sirdar, decided to take the Presbyterian Mission school authorities to court, accusing them of forcing his son to turn from the faith of his fathers to become a convert to Christianity.

The case, naturally, was the talk of the neighbourhood. The missionary in charge, who lived in another area, was summoned to appear, along with the headmaster and others, but the case was eventually dismissed, mainly on the evidence of the boy himself. He declared that no pressure had been put on him to become a believer in Jesus Christ. 'Not because of the padré sahib but by reading this Book,' holding up the New Testament, 'I believe in Christ. So let the padré sahib go,' he said, and Sundar said the same.

The dismissal of the case by the magistrate did not dismiss the matter from the minds of the local community. The Christian minority had a hard time of it. Things were made so difficult for them that a number of them moved away. And the school was doomed. Most of the local Sikhs and Hindus withdrew their children from it, and within a matter of weeks it was closed down.

Sher Singh, anxious that Sundar's education should not be hindered, and glad, perhaps, of the opportunity to get him away from the village where he was rather in disgrace, agreed to send him to the Presbyterian High School in Ludhiana.

To Sundar this must have seemed the best thing that could happen to him. To be sent into a Christian community where he would be free to express his faith and live according to it was all he could have desired at that point. He would have a good education based on Christian principles, and be living in a Christian hostel with boys like himself. So he must have expected.

The missionaries themselves received him with great understanding, and in order to avoid making trouble with his family arranged for food to be specially prepared for him that would in no way go against Sikh customs. What they could not so easily control was the talk and behaviour of the boys in the hostel. Sundar never disclosed what it was that so deeply disturbed him, but he was shocked to find that the schoolmates he had expected to share his devotion to Christ were Christian in name only. He had had no close connection with Christians except with the teachers in the primary school, and with Sirdar, whose faith was as bright as his own. The disillusionment of that term in the school at Ludhiana was so great that he went back to his home saying he did not want to return.

His family members were delighted. This, they thought, meant that he had given up the idea of becoming a Christian. They welcomed him back warmly, until they discovered that he was still reading his Bible, still praying secretly to Jesus, still determined not to go to the temples or take any part in Sikh or Hindu worship. Then their attitude changed towards him, and they tried all means to make him change his mind. They let him know what it felt like to be excluded from the family gatherings at meal times, to eat his food alone on the verandah while the rest of them sat round in a circle, dipping their morsels of rice or chappati into the various spices on the tray before them. Some of them jeered at him; others tried to argue him out of his convictions. At one stage he was sent to stay with a relative in the service of the local Maharajah, and was taken for an audience with the great man. The Maharajah started by speaking persuasively to him, dwelling on the dignity and honour of being a Sikh, and one of the family of Singh, a lion, of carrying the Five Signs of the Sikh — the dagger, the bracelet, the shorts, the comb, and above all, the long hair which had never been cut from birth. But when the boy, standing politely before him, quietly adhered to his faith in Jesus Christ, he turned on him in scorn, telling him he was not a lion at all but a jackal.

The humiliating interview concluded with his being contemptuously dismissed, which only added to the evident displeasure of his relative. For a fifteen-year-old boy such pressure from various sources could have proved strong enough to silence him, if not to alter his inner convictions.

But in Sundar's case, it had the opposite effect. As he studied the Gospels and the Acts of the Apostles, read how the wonderful Christ whom he had seen with his own eyes had himself endured shame as well as suffering, how his disciples had actually rejoiced at being 'counted worthy of suffering disgrace in the Name,' there was born in Sundar the desire to suffer also — to suffer for the sake of Christ. As for one day undergoing the initiation ceremony that would mark him out, not only as having attained manhood, but primarily as being a Sikh, he could not and would not go through with it. It was not that he wanted to disclaim his race and his ancestry. What he disclaimed was the Sikh religion. In spite of the disillusionment of his time in the school in Ludhiana, in spite of the threats, scorn and ill-treatment he had encountered, in spite even of the persuasions and entreaties of his father and older members of the family, he knew that nothing could obliterate the memory of the living Christ who had been revealed to him. It was Christ who claimed his allegiance, and it was Christ who should have it.

Something had to be done to make it evident, to convince his family that he had relinquished for ever the Sikh religion, that he had seen Jesus Christ, and was determined to follow him. As he thought about it he realised there was one way in which he could it. By one simple action he could demonstrate that he was freeing himself forever from the binding traditions of his race. It was a simple action, but it would be irrevocable, and he realised that it would plunge him into difficulties far greater than any he had yet encountered. But whatever the outcome, he made up his mind to do it.

He took a pair of scissors and cut off his hair.

TO SATISFY THE SOUL

In comparison with this big world, the human heart is only a small thing. Though the world is so large, it is utterly unable to satisfy this tiny heart. Man's ever-growing soul and its capacities can only be satisfied in the infinite God.

As water is restless until it reaches its level, so the soul has not peace until it rests in God.

With and Without Christ

3

To the Sikh in the Punjab long hair was the chief of the Five Signs, his glory, the *Kev* which he wore tied in a knob at the top of his head. The bracelet, the shorts, the comb and the dagger that distinguished him were as nothing without it. In his sacred book, the *Granth*, he was instructed never to cut his hair and as a devout Sikh he never did so. His beard, often luxuriant (though very uncomfortable in the hot, dusty weather) remained untrimmed, but it was the long hair of his poll that crowned it all. A Sikh with his hair shorn was a Sikh no longer. He was cut off from his religion, his community and his family.

The shock of horror with which Sher Singh saw what Sundar had done was followed by an exhibition of anger such as Sundar had never witnessed before. His father was furious, and without hesitation ordered him out of the home, telling him he was no longer a member of the family. He had disgraced it. He was an outcaste, had no right in the Singh courtyard. He must get out — and get out quickly.

Sundar knew there was nothing for it but to obey.

He did so immediately. With nothing but the clothes he was wearing, and clutching his New Testament, he went through the gate of the courtyard, not knowing where he would go or what he would do. No home would be open to him, he knew that. The news of what he had done would spread like wildfire through the village. He was an outcaste, one to whom, in the language all Indians understood, 'the water and the pipe were forbidden'. He was cut off completely from the social intercourse which the smoking of the pipe symbolised, and no one would give him a drink of water, for his lips would soil the vessel from which he drank. He knew all this theoretically, had taken it for granted when it applied to the outcastes whom he saw every day, sweeping the streets. Now it applied to him — but with one big difference.

Unlike the sweepers who lived in a different world, had their own community, were accustomed from birth to poverty and deprivation, he was alone. There was no one to whom he could turn. He had no community.

He walked across to a tree, and sat down under it, shivering slightly.

Never before had he been in such a situation, without food, without shelter, without adequate clothing. He thought of the warmth of the family home, of the group gathered around the food tray, of the pile of bedding in his room — all so familiar, all within a few hundred yards of where he was now huddled — yet all irrevocably cut off from him.

The realisation could have filled him with dismay, but he found it was having the opposite effect. Although physically he was suffering, emotionally he was conscious, not only of peace, but of an inexpressible joy. It was different from the memorable night a year before, when he had actually seen the living

Christ. This time he saw nothing, but the sense of Christ's presence overwhelmed him. Not for anything would he have changed his present situation for the comfort of his luxurious home, where every physical need had been met, but his mind and heart had been in turmoil. Although outwardly he was in distress, inwardly he was experiencing such a deep fellowship with his Master that he often referred to it as his first night in heaven. He had entered a new dimension of spiritual experience. He was suffering not only for, but with his Master, and knew what was meant by the words 'he regarded disgrace for the sake of Christ as of greater value than the treasures of Egypt' (Heb. 11:26).

So the hours of the night passed in blissful contentment. But as dawn broke, the practical aspect of his situation had to be faced. He could not remain there forever, under a tree in the village. Where should he go, and what should he do? He knew that the homes of the whole Sikh community would be closed to him, and they were the only people on whom he would have a natural claim. To look for help from Hindus or Muslims was out of the question. Only one avenue seemed open to him. He must go to the Christians.

It would be useless to approach any of those living locally. They were the sweeper caste and had already suffered because of the closing of the mission school. They would be afraid to help him, even if they were able, and it is doubtful if the thought of appealing to them ever occurred to Sundar. The nearest place where he could hope to find a refuge was Rupar, a large village about thirty miles away, where he knew there was a Presbyterian Mission centre. He decided that he would go and explain his position to the pastor there. So he set off on the journey — but not before he had a final contact with one member of the family. His sister-in-law, unsmiling, put some food under a

37

verandah, the place where outcastes were allowed to eat, and indicated it was for him.

It was very humiliating, and Sundar felt it keenly. To find himself classed in this way with the despised lowest castes, scorned by his own family, hurt him more than he would have expected. The mutual respect and acceptance between members of a community is rarely appreciated until it is withdrawn. The shock of expulsion from his home after he had cut off his hair was dramatic, but not entirely unexpected, and he could stand up to it. The night out in the open, witnessed by no human eye, had been exultant. But now things were returning to normal. Life was stirring in the village, and the thought of startled or contemptuous glances as he was seen picking up the food from under the verandah almost deterred him from doing so. Only his hunger, and uncertainty about where his next meal would come from, decided him. Sundar took the food, and set off for Rupar.

Several hours later he arrived at the home of the Presbyterian pastor there, the Rev. P. C. Uppal, who when he knew the identity of the boy who had arrived on his verandah, received him immediately with the utmost kindness. He himself had been driven from his Hindu home when he asserted his faith in Christ, and knew the hazards faced by those who dared to do so from a similar background. When, shortly after his arrival, Sundar began to have violent spasms of pain, the pastor suspected what had happened. So did Sundar. The food he had been given was poisoned.

He knew that the use of poison to do away with those who openly turned from their old religion to follow another was by no means uncommon. But it had not occurred to him, until he began to feel ill on his way to Rupar, that this is what might have happened to him. (He learned later that the other Sikh

38

boy, Sirdar, who had also become a Christian, had been killed in this way.)

Within a short time Sundar was bleeding from nose and mouth and Mr Uppal sent an urgent message to the dispenser in the local hospital to come at once, while Mrs Uppal did what she could to make Sundar comfortable. But when the dispenser arrived and saw Sundar, and heard his story, he refused to treat him.

'He's going to die,' he told the Uppals. 'This is a very bad case of poisoning and he can't recover. If I do anything for him he'll die anyway, but I'll get the blame for his death.' To humour the boy who pleaded for the last chapter of Mark's Gospel to be read aloud, he waited to hear it, said the story of Christ's resurrection was very far-fetched and went away. He would be back again next morning, he said, to see the patient, but it was obvious that he expected Sundar to be dead by that time.

The next morning he arrived as he had promised, and to his amazement he saw Sundar lying on the verandah, weak but free from pain, and even able to smile at him. Then he learned what had happened.

During the night Sundar had become convinced that it was not God's will for him to die, but that he should live to tell others about Christ. Gathering together what strength he could muster, he had prayed that he might be healed. He knew that God was able to heal him, and God had done so.

The dispenser's astonishment was evident, and he did not try to hide it. Yes, he admitted, it was a miracle. He had not expected to see Sundar alive again, yet here he was, healed of his pain and just like anyone else who was recovering from a severe illness. He looked at the New Testament with a new respect, asked for a copy and went away thoughtfully to read

39

it. It was a turning point in his life, though neither he nor Sundar realised it at the time.

For Sundar this was a landmark in his spiritual experience. The conviction that it was God's will that he should live and not die was accompanied by his own prayer for healing. Not fatalism but faith released the divine power that brought it about. 'And these signs will accompany those who believe...' he had heard as the last chapter of Mark's Gospel was read, and the list of miracles referred to had included sick people who would be healed. '...those who believe.' He had believed that miracles could happen but now he knew they did.

Sundar made a quick but uneventful recovery in the Uppals' home, comforted by their kindness. Meanwhile Mr Uppal had been in touch with the American Presbyterian missionaries about him. Obviously Sundar could not remain in Rupar. It was too near to his own home, and it would be impossible to protect him from his family. In any case, there was his future to consider and it was decided that the best thing would be for him to go to the Boarding School in Ludhiana until he was sixteen — the age at which he would be considered an adult, and legally free to decide for himself what he would do. So to Ludhiana he went.

The first person he met there was his former fellow-student in the primary school at Rampur, the son of the headmaster who had helped him with Bible study. This boy had been specially summoned to the Principal's study in order that he might welcome Sundar and befriend him in his difficult situation. The members of the staff of the Presbyterian Mission were deeply concerned about this new arrival, and did all they could think of to ease things for him. They were aware of the vulnerability of his position, and knew there were limits to the protection they could afford. He had come to them of his own free will, and humanly speaking they had saved his life, for had they not taken him in when he arrived at the Mission in Rupar he would have died. The dispenser at the hospital could vouch for that. But if he yielded to persuasion or pressure from his family to return to them the missionaries could do nothing about it.

It must have been a tense time for them when one day Sher Singh, accompanied by other members of his family, arrived at the school and demanded to see his son. There was nothing for it but to admit him, although they refused to allow the others to come in and eventually they left the premises. Sher Singh himself, however, was taken to where Sundar was talking with his friend and the scene that followed was so touching that his friend never forgot it. Neither did Sundar himself for as he saw his father, looking drawn and rather haggard, and heard his voice pleading for him to return to his home, he found himself longing to do so. He was not happy in the school. The rhythm of life was different from that to which he had been accustomed. The routine in the compound of the Singhs followed much the same free and easy pattern each day, but it was coloured by comings and goings, by quarrels, or cheerful rowdy games amongst the boys. And it was always possible for him to slip away to a secluded spot to meditate or pray or read his New Testament.

At school it was different. The regimentation of life with its set time for lessons, for recreation, for meals, for sport, and for worship services irked one of his temperament, and although he fitted into the schedule without complaint he was not at ease. Now seeing his father almost in tears as he pleaded with him to come

41

home and give up the idea of being a Christian, Sundar was nearer to succumbing than he had ever been. As his father reminded him of his mother's love for him, of her devout life, he remembered the happy days of his childhood and his eyes misted over. How could he turn away from all the love and security his family offered him? And how could he hurt his father, whose grief was so obvious, by refusing his pleas?

The clinging tendrils of family relationships and his father's love were very strong, but even as he hesitated to answer, he realised that something else was stronger. The memory of his vision of Christ was as clear as ever. He could not deny that nor the consciousness of the change within himself. As he looked at his father, saw the earnestness of his desire that his son should return, he knew what he had to do.

'I can't. I can't,' he said in an anguished voice. 'I am a Christian and I always want to be one.' Then he added 'I love Christ.'

His father, seeing Sundar's determination, fought back his tears and became quite bitter before eventually leaving. He implied that Sundar had not heard the last of the matter, and a few days later a little crowd of relatives came to the school and had to be forcibly restrained from entering and getting hold of him. It happened two or three times before the term ended and the Presbyterian missionaries wondered where they could send him when school closed. It had to be somewhere far enough away from Rampur to prevent the militant Singhs from getting at him again and somewhere where he would be cared for among Christians.

After some discussion they decided that the best place for him would be Sabathu.

In Sabathu, a small town situated some twenty miles from the city of Simla, the American Presbyterian Mission had a hospital for the treatment of sufferers from leprosy. There on the compound a place could be found for this earnest lad to live among the staff. His story was already becoming known, and the missionaries felt a special responsibility for him. He could remain in the hospital compound at least until he was sixteen, when he himself must decide what he would do. Suggestions might be made regarding his future career, and help would be forthcoming along certain lines, but the final decision would rest with him. Before he was sixteen no decisive action could be taken anyway.

So to Sabathu Sundar went. At last he experienced not only inward peace but outward calm as well. Away from the strain of antagonism in his own home, and away from the strictly organised life at school, he was free to spend his time as he pleased, living with people who went about their work cheerfully and accepted his presence among them without question.

Those were weeks of rest and renewal for him after the varied tensions of the past months. The hospital was built on the edge of a pine forest where he would wander at will, satisfying a deep-seated desire for solitude and reviving the impressions made on him as a child, when his mother took him from time to time to see the old *sadhu*. The longing for peace, the yearning for Something or Someone unseen that he had sensed in them both had been passed on to him, but now there was a difference. He experienced the peace they had been seeking, he knew the One they had unknowingly been reaching out for behind the curtain of sense. He had seen him and he knew him — but he longed to know him better. There in the stillness of the forest, the silence broken only by the songs of birds or the rustlings of little creatures moving in the undergrowth, Sundar pored over his Bible, leaning

43

against a tree meditating on what he had read, opening his young heart to its influences.

It was a period in which his overstrung emotions were relieved, and when he could say with the psalmist of old 'He makes me lie down in green pastures, he leads me beside quiet waters, he restores my soul.' He was consciously preparing himself for the next step in his spiritual pilgrimage — his baptism. Again and again he read the Gospels, picturing the man Christ Jesus going to John the Baptist by the river Jordan, taking his place among those who came confessing their sins, though he had no sin to confess. He followed this Man of Galilee through all the experiences of that matchless life, moved not only by the miracles and teaching, but by the steadfast progress to the cross that Jesus knew awaited him. The desire to suffer for Christ, already born in him, deepened. It was not sufficient to serve him; he wanted to endure pain and privation for his sake.

Meanwhile, the time was drawing near when he would reach his sixteenth birthday, and be legally free to be baptised. He had made his desire to take this step very clear and Dr Fife, the headmaster of the boarding school in Ludhiana, made the necessary arrangements. He wrote to Mr Redland of the Church Missionary Society in Simla, introducing Sundar and explaining his situation. During quite a long interview Mr Redland questioned the tall well-built boy before him on many matters of faith, all of which he answered clearly and convincingly. Especially, he had an unusually intimate and accurate knowledge of the life and teaching of Christ. The person of Christ evidently filled his vision. Without the slightest reservation Mr Redland pronounced him ready for baptism and on the following day, the third of September 1905, his sixteenth birthday, Sundar was baptised.

The final step had been taken. When he cut off his hair he cut himself off from the Sikh religion and everything connected with it, including his own family. When he was baptised in St Thomas's Church in Simla, he was openly identifying himself with the Christian faith and all that it stood for. Now the way was clear for him to decide what he would do in the future.

In a way that decision had already been made. He had told Mr Redman, during the interview preceding his baptism, that he knew what he must do. He must preach. An inner compulsion, allied to the last command of the risen Christ to his disciples, convinced him of that. The only question was the method by which he should do it. Should he follow the usual pattern in India and go through the long process of training in a theological college established by the missionaries? It would have been the simplest and most natural thing to do for the missionaries had proved his best friends during the tumultuous months through which he had passed. But something held him back.

It was the memory of his mother. Her influence on him as a child had helped to mould his character and his desires, so that the decision he made did not go against the grain. 'Don't be careless and worldly like your brothers,' she had often said. 'Far better to renounce the world and seek the way of true enlightenment.'

He did not need to seek the way of enlightenment, but it would be in keeping with her earnest desire for him that he should go on the path of renunciation. He remembered the intimation of the old *sadhu* in the jungle that he himself would one day be a *sadhu* — one who had renounced family, money, property, everything, and who went on a wandering life, dependent on others for his daily food. And he knew from his study of the Gospels that when Christ sent forth his disciples to preach and to heal, he told them to take nothing with them.

Quietly he decided that this is what he would do. He would become a *sadhu*. He would go from place to place in the manner of the *sadhus*, but not on pilgrimages to shrines and temples. He would go to preach. He would be a Christian *sadhu*.

He knew, true son of India that he was, that in the saffron robe of the *sadhu* doors would be open to him that would otherwise be closed. He would not be qualified to preach in the churches but, clad in the robe of one who was known to have taken the path of renunciation, he could reach the villagers, the common people, even the high-caste women secluded in their zenanas.

At the age of sixteen, before he was entangled with any of the things the world holds dear, he made his decision — and stuck to it.

It was back in Sabathu that the thought crystallised into reality. He had returned there after his baptism, and remained for a month, gradually disposing of his belongings and preparing himself for what lay ahead. He spent hours in the forest praying and meditating. At other times he went to a high vantage point to scan the distant horizons. In every direction there were vast areas where the name of Christ was not known. For hundreds of miles to the south lay the plains of India shimmering in the heat. Westward too, the plains spread as far as the eye could see, and beyond to the land of Afghanistan. But as he looked to the north-east it was different. On the far horizon what appeared to be a large grey mass of cloud rose straight up from the plateau. Only the rays of the setting sun lit up the tips of that mass to reveal the dazzling

46

whiteness of eternal snows. It was the Himalayan range, and beyond those mighty mountains lay the remote and isolated land of Tibet.

He must go there too, one day. But first he must go to his own people.

On 6 October 1905, his feet bare, wearing the simple saffron robe that marked him off as one vowed to a religious life, a blanket over his shoulder and his New Testament in his hand, Sundar Singh the *sadhu*, bade farewell to his friends in Sabathu and set off for the villages of India.

EACH TO HIS CALLING

Everyone should follow his calling and carry out his work according to his God-given gifts and capacities. The same breath is blown into flute, cornet and bagpipe, but different music is produced according to the different instruments. In the same way the one Spirit works in us, God's children, but different results are produced, and God is glorified through them according to each one's temperament and personality.

With and Without Christ

Chapter

4

When Sundar set out that October day in 1905, bare-footed and wearing his saffron robe, it is doubtful whether he had any clear idea of where he would eventually go, except that he seems to have had the mountainous areas of Afghanistan and Kashmir in mind. But first he went towards his own home village of Rampur.

He went slowly, entering village after village on the way to stop and preach wherever there was an opportunity. The appearance of a tall, well-built young sadhu in a clean robe attracted a fair amount of attention. Initial reaction to him was usually favourable, for not many sadhus were either clean or young. All too often they repelled rather than attracted. Even before he started to preach he was sometimes offered food, although he never asked for it. He had made up his mind that he would not beg. He would eat whatever food was offered to him, but if none was forthcoming he would go without. He would trust God to supply him with what he needed.

When he started to speak and talk about Jesus

Christ, reactions varied. In some cases the listeners assumed that this Jesus was yet another god to be added to the existing hierarchy of Hindu deities. Sundar's claim that he had actually seen him, that Christ had completely changed him and given him peace and joy for hopelessness and despair, had no more effect than to arouse a passing interest. And since the young sadhu had already taken the path of renunciation, it was an act of merit to provide him with food and shelter. By renouncing everything, including caste, he was acceptable to all — unless there were those among his listeners who realised that he was a Christian. Then the reaction was very different.

A Christian! One of those religionists who were mainly drawn from the outcastes, followers of the religion of the people of the west. A sadhu who was a Christian! Out with him!

As Sundar made his way from village to village, there were many nights when he had to sleep outside in a disused hut or under a tree. On one occasion, hungry as well as weary, he was almost yielding to a bout of self-pity when suddenly he felt a surge of joy welling up within him to such an extent that he burst out into song. When he recounted the experience years later he did so with a wry smile. He knew he had no singing voice and wondered what the villagers had made of it. At any rate it woke some of them up, for after he had been singing for some time two of them came to see what it was all about. Quite simply he explained to them that having had nothing to eat all day he was too hungry to sleep but that he was so happy he could not help singing.

Even if they could not understand why anyone who was hungry could be happy, they could appreciate the reason for his sleeplessness.

'We didn't know,' they said apologetically, evidently rather ashamed that one who had chosen the path of renunciation should have fared so badly in their village. They went off immediately to get him some food which he received gratefully, and after he had eaten it he wrapped his blanket around him and fell fast asleep. It was an occasion when quite unintentionally he sang for his supper.

It was with mixed feelings that he drew near to his own home village, wondering what sort of reception he would get. To his surprise the people he met, on recognising him, greeted him warmly. The traders in the bazaar, the workers in the fields, even some of his former school mates, far from revealing any scorn or antagonism, all appeared to accept his new role and listened to him without argument.

When he reached his own home however, there was no such response to his appearance. At first his father refused even to see him, but then, without a smile told him he had disgraced the family by becoming a Christian, that he could come in for the night but must leave at daybreak next morning. He indicated where Sundar could sit while the family had their meal — away from the rest of them, by himself. Then he came across, put some food down for Sundar to eat and held aloft a vessel of water.

'Hold out your hands,' he said, and Sundar knew what was meant. He was to cup his hands together to drink the water that would be poured into them. No vessel would be given to him to drink from — he would pollute it.

It was the method used to give drink to the untouchables and it was too much for Sundar. He broke down. With tears running down his cheeks and a choking voice he thanked his father, said goodbye and left. Again he slept under a tree in his own village, outside his home. Analysing his own feelings he realised that though there was grief that the father who had once loved him now appeared to hate him, his underlying peace of heart remained. 'My peace I give to you,' the Lord Jesus had said to his disciples on the very night before he was crucified, and that gift of peace had been given to him too. And nothing could take it away.

Although that underlying peace never changed, there is no doubt that he had many periods of despondency. On one occasion he had been walking all day and arrived at a village in the evening very weary. It started to rain and as he walked along the main street several people came forward to offer him hospitality. They thought he was a Hindu sadhu, but when he spoke of Jesus they turned quite violently against him. He had no option but to get out of the village, and stumbled along, pursued by the indignant shouts of some of the men.

The rain continued and he was wet through when at last he found a derelict hut and went inside, thankful for a roof over his head. He was so tired he fell asleep almost as soon as he lay down and did not wake up until dawn was beginning to break. Then, just as he was about to stretch his legs, he saw beside him a dark form on the ground. Peering through the dim light he saw with horror that it was a huge cobra curled up on part of the blanket in which he had been sleeping.

Holding his breath he edged away and dashed out of the hut as fast as his legs would carry him. But having got outside he thought of his blanket. He needed that blanket. It was absolutely indispensable on cold nights, some of which he might have to spend out of doors. With an earnest prayer he turned back, crept into the hut and very cautiously eased the blanket from under the weight of that huge black cobra. If the creature awoke and struck out at him suddenly he knew it could mean his death. But the snake merely rolled over a little and went on sleeping.

As he travelled he learned how to cope, among other things, with the difficulty of keeping clean. Daily ablutions, including washing his hair, were not always easy to perform, nor was the washing of his clothes. It was noticed that his saffron robe, unlike that of most of the sadhus, was always spotless. He found means of washing it and waiting for it to dry while wrapped in his blanket. Sometimes he had to put it on while it was still wet. But at whatever inconvenience to himself, the habits of cleanliness ingrained in him from childhood were maintained.

Other habits too. His days started with hours of prayer and meditation, continuing the custom started as a child under the influence of his mother.

He learned to adapt his physical appetite to the provision forthcoming — and to augment it when necessary with such fruits, leaves and roots as were available and digestible. Very early in his life this young disciple of Jesus Christ was bringing his natural appetites under control, freeing his active mind to assimilate and store impressions which were later to be used in his preaching. For, like his Master, Sundar spoke in parables.

One such parable which he often used was built on an incident of which he heard when in Kashmir. The owner of several hundred sheep, on counting them over as they were brought home by their shepherds at night, found that some were missing, and he determined to find them. His problem was that the sheep did not know him and therefore would not follow him. They would be afraid of a strange man, but he reasoned with himself that they would not be afraid of another sheep. So he wrapped a sheepskin around

53

himself and went to find them. As he heard their bleating he was directed to them, and when they saw what appeared to be another sheep they followed, and so were brought into the fold.

'So it was with God — he came and lived among us, clothed in our humanity. Christ, as man, became as one of us one of whom we are not afraid, and so he can lead us into his fold.'

On another occasion on a railway station, he saw a Brahmin who had been taken seriously ill and needed water. However, when the station-master brought him some in a cup he refused to drink it. He rejected the foreign vessel in which it came. Not until water was poured into his own brass bowl would he receive it.

'So the Hindu is more prepared to receive the Water of Life when it is offered to him in a vessel he can accept. The sadhu is a familiar figure and gains a readier hearing everywhere than the foreigner, or even the Indian who adopts the western manner of life and general approach. The Water is the same, but the vessel in which it is offered is different. If the vessel is acceptable it is more likely that the Water will be received.'

That first journey of his took him through Baluchistan to the borders of Afghanistan, along the famous Khyber Pass into the country itself. It was here that on a later visit, he had an experience which again threatened his life, but in which the living Presence of God turned the tide that was against him.

He had reached the town of Jalalabad and among that Muslim population his preaching about Jesus, accepted by Islam as one of the prophets, was listened to quietly enough until it became evident that he was being proclaimed as God. Immediately the mood of his listeners changed into open hostility and he was warned that if he did not get out quickly he would be killed. Night was coming on, and he made his way to the only place open to him — the *serai* where the caravans of animals and their drivers from Central Asia lodged for the night. There was very little shelter from the bitter cold, and as it had been raining Sundar slept very uneasily if at all. Early in the morning he got up and was drying his robe by the fire that had been kindled, when he looked and saw at the entrance of the *serai* a group of the very men who had been threatening him the night before.

It was an alarming moment. He wondered if they had come to carry out their threat to take him off and kill him. Instead, they stood there looking at him with amazement. What they had expected to see if he was alive at all, was a shuddering half-dead creature, scarcely able to stand. What they saw was a tall well-built, bearded youth obviously in good health, half-clad in his robe which he was drying by the fire.

Perhaps they saw more than that. Perhaps there was something about that figure which slightly awed them. At any rate, they stood and talked together, then one of them came forward and to Sundar's surprise bowed to him. Then he admitted that they had come to kill him off if he was not already dead from exposure, but on seeing him alive and evidently well they had realised that Allah had preserved him. That being the case, he was urged to come back with them and tell them the message he had come to deliver.

This surprising turn of events resulted in Sundar's remaining for about a week as a guest in the house of the leader of the group. To what extent he was able effectively to convey his message is uncertain since he did not speak their language, but their whole attitude towards him had changed. They recognised in him one who was preserved by the Supreme Being whom they knew as Allah. The presence of God with his servant had given him an inner power and dignity which subdued his opponents and commanded their respect. It was to happen many times in the years that lay ahead.

Sundar returned to Sabathu from his first preaching pilgrimage much thinner than when he set out, and was glad of a refuge in the area with which he had become so familiar. It was while he was there that he met a wealthy American, S. E. Stokes, who had come to India fired with the desire to live for Christ in that country. Immediately a friendship was forged between the two. Stokes was reminded of the famous St Francis of Assisi, whose life had inspired his decision to come to India, but of whom Sundar had never heard.

'Francis of Assisi was born in Italy some eight hundred years ago,' Stokes told Sundar. 'He was born into a very wealthy family so he had plenty of money, and was a very popular young man. But when he was about twenty-two years old he started thinking about God. One day he heard a preacher speak from the tenth chapter of Matthew's Gospel, where Jesus told his disciples to go out and preach, warning people to turn from their wrong-doing and come to God. Jesus also told them to heal those who were ill, to cast out devils and to do good. And he told them to take no money but to eat such food as was given to them wherever they went.

'Francis knew that this was what Christ was now telling him to do and he obeyed. He gave away all his money and possessions and went out preaching. But he did not only preach. He helped people in a practical way, caring for them when they were sick, sharing his food with beggars, helping the weak. He was entirely different from the priests in the churches who did not move a finger to help anyone. He had a wonderful power over animals too, seeing them as God's creatures just as we are. None of them, even the fiercest, ever hurt him. So eventually Francis became famous and other young men inspired by his example followed him. He founded the religious order called the Franciscans.'

The resemblance of Sundar's chosen manner of life to that of Francis of Assisi was obvious. As Stokes talked to him and heard of the opportunities he had, the doors that opened to him as he moved from place to place, as well as the hardships he had to suffer, and as he saw the joy this young Sikh had in serving his Master, Stokes was stirred. He decided to join Sundar and take to the Indian road as a sadhu.

So it came about that for several months Sundar and the American travelled together, sharing the same food, enduring the same privations. Inevitably Sundar had to take the lead, for he knew the language and the customs of his own people. The marvel was that the American, coming from such an entirely different background, adapted himself so well to a manner of life that was hard even for an Indian, and that the two of them merged together so harmoniously. The ardour of their spirits bound them together. And eventually it was Sundar not Stokes who broke down physically. He was suddenly seized with acute internal pain and very soon was feverish and shaking with ague. He struggled on till he could walk no longer and collapsed on the path.

It was an alarming situation for Stokes who bent over him trying to make him comfortable, and enquiring earnestly, 'How are you?' He never forgot the reply he received. A faint smile came over Sundar's boyish face and he murmured,

'I am very happy. How sweet it is to suffer for his sake!'

'How sweet it is to suffer for his sake!' That was the keynote of Sundar's life. Unlike the 'holy men' who deliberately inflicted pain on themselves by lying on spikes, or walling themselves into a cell, or in some other way sought to gain merit by means of personal physical torment, he did not seek suffering. He did not relish it more than any other healthily-minded person. But he was learning to accept it even with joy when it came in the course of his service for Christ.

Stokes looked at his young companion and realised that he was physically incapable of moving. Something must be done to get him to a place where he could rest and be nursed back to health. Learning that there was a European living not far away, Stokes went to him and asked for his help. History does not relate the first reactions of the man when confronted by a white-skinned sadhu in a saffron robe who spoke in fluent English with an American accent! But he acceded to the request for help and had Sundar brought to his home. With rest, good food and suitable medication, the young Sikh recovered quickly and before long he and Stokes were back on the road. But their brief stay in the home of that European led to his putting his faith in Christ.

Returning to Sabathu, they found there was a need for help in the hospital for leprosy patients and worked there for a while until, hearing that plague had broken out on the plains, they went down to the plague camp itself to serve like Francis of Assisi before them by nursing the sick and dying.

It was their last period of working together, for although they kept in touch for some time, and usually spent a short period each summer taking crippled boys to a camp in the hills, their paths separated.

Stokes went to America and to England, recruiting young men to join a brotherhood to work rather on Franciscan lines in India. And Sundar, responding to the urge that he had been aware of while waiting for his baptism, turned his steps at last towards the land that lay behind that great grey mass on the northern horizon — Tibet.

MAN MUST WORSHIP

You will hardly find men who do not worship God or some power. If atheistic thinkers or scientists, filled with the materialistic outlook, do not worship God, they often tend to worship great men and heroes or some ideal which they have exalted into a Power. Buddha did not teach anything about God. The result was, his followers began to worship him. In China the people began to worship ancestors, as they were not taught to worship God. Even illiterate people are found worshipping some power or some spirit. In short, man cannot but worship. This desire for worship, from which man cannot get away, has been created in him by his Creator, so that led by this desire, he may have communion with his Creator.

Reality and Religion

Chapter

5

There is probably no area on the earth's surface that has stirred and challenged human endeavour more than the vast tableland of Tibet in Central Asia. With the mighty Himalayan range of mountains forming a natural buttress against the teeming millions of India, and hundreds of miles of bleak windswept plateau stretching eastward to the thickly populated cities and plains of China, it was an almost impregnable fortress at the time when Sundar's eyes turned towards it. Intrepid mountaineers and explorers had tried to climb its heights and discover its secrets. Politicians had made treaties, and a few messengers of the Cross had made hazardous efforts to establish the name of Jesus there.

In 1846 the Abbés Huc and Gabet had actually reached Lhasa after an epic journey from north-west China, a journey that lasted a year and a half. Their desire was to 'preach Christ crucified for the salvation of mankind'. But although they were well received by the Tibetans, they were compelled to leave Lhasa after two months. The Chinese ambassador was the one who brought it about, but the Abbés saw beyond the human agent to 'the enemy of all good who was hard at work to ruin our prospects and to remove us from a country he seems to have chosen for the seat of his empire.'

Fifty years later a Canadian doctor and her Dutch husband, after living for a year or two in a lamasery in Kum Bum, also in north-west China, set off with their baby boy for the interior. It was a tragic journey of incredible danger and hardship from which Dr Susie Rijnhart returned alone having accomplished apparently nothing, though her story challenged and inspired others to go to the Tibetans. At the same time members of the China Inland Mission and the Christian Missionary Alliance were settling in towns on the Sino-Tibetan border. But although there were Chinese and tribal people who responded to their message, their efforts to reach Tibetans themselves with the gospel were repulsed again and again.

The priesthood reigned unopposed over both the nomads and the villagers in their little flat-roofed homes scattered thinly across the vast tablelands — homes that were overshadowed by lamaseries where the lamas intoned their prayers and beat their gongs. The lamaseries were the centres of religious life, drawing all their support from the laity. Unlike the animistic tribes-people whose deities were mainly localised, the Tibetans were held together by a centuries' old system which centred in the Dalai Lama in Lhasa, and nothing it seemed could change their allegiance to him, their king and their god.

Sundar, of course, knew nothing of all this. As he looked at the vast range of the Himalayas, rearing like a great wall on the northern horizon, he had no idea how many people lived beyond those rugged mountains. He only knew that when the snows melted some of them came down the trade routes to barter their goods, hardy, robust men, bold-eyed and cheerful but very dirty. And they were superstitious. Handling their rosaries they murmured 'O Mani Padme Hum, O Mani Padme Hum' over and over again, in the confidence that by doing so they were accumulating the merit necessary to ensure a better birth in their next reincarnation. Some of them carried prayer wheels in the folds of their garments which they produced from time to time, twirling them rapidly thereby producing prayers at the rate the wheel rotated, while their minds were occupied with other matters. Their shaven-headed priests the lamas moved among them, distinctive in their maroon-coloured robes, venerated and supported and obviously not expected to do any work. As winter approached they all disappeared again up the passes into their snow-bound land.

Sundar's eyes had turned again and again to those mountains, and now he believed the time had come to go and proclaim as best he could, the message of forgiveness and eternal salvation to the men and women who lived there.

He was nineteen years old when he set off up one of the passes along which some Indian traders were travelling. Arriving at the little town of Poo, in the Himalayan foothills, he learned that two Europeans were living there who had come to the border to establish a Christian mission, and to reach Tibetans with the gospel. They were members of the Moravian Mission which had been established in Ladakh, Kashmir, some fifty years earlier. The original aim of the Mission had been to get into Tibet, but they had been foiled in their efforts and had eventually settled on the border.

The missionaries in Poo were learning the Tibetan language and when Sundar told them of his desire to take the gospel into Tibet they encouraged him to remain with them for a short time and to learn some rudiments of the language and prepare himself for what he might encounter. When eventually he left them to go further into the mountains a young local Christian in their employ was sent with him. Sundar was very grateful for his companionship. He was going among a people whose customs and manner of life were entirely strange to him, and without the aid of one who knew them he would undoubtedly have fared far worse than he did on that first journey.

He had to get accustomed to their food, which was very indigestible, consisting mainly of ground parched barley, butter that was usually rancid and tea with salt in it. Worse than that, from his point of view, the Tibetans evidently never washed. Their faces and hands were grimy and as they rubbed rancid butter on their skin to shield it from the cold, the odour from their bodies smote him. And when they realised that he had come to preach a different religion from their own, their uninhibited show of interest soon turned to angry hostility. For these people he soon discovered were fierce religionists. They submitted gladly to the rule of the lamas, the priesthood that bound them together like a web that stretched from border to border of their vast land. They had been warned that a foreign power was planning to destroy their religion and they were prepared to resist it with all their might.

That first journey lasted a few weeks and on the whole Sundar and his companion encountered no violent opposition. The lamas warned the people against their preaching, but otherwise the hardships they endured were mainly those that anyone walking over the rugged mountains would encounter. And at one lamasery to their surprise, the head lama welcomed them and listened intently to what they had to say. Sundar had been eased gently into the pioneering work among Tibetans that was to become so distinctive a part of his life. From then on, although he continued to move from village to village, and sometimes into the towns of India, he always had in mind the time when the snows in the foothills of the Himalayas would be melting. Year after year found him moving with the streams of traders and pilgrims making their way up the passes into the remote lands of the Himalayas.

But before this became a dominating factor in his life there came an interlude which tested his calibre as a Christian and revealed to him afresh weaknesses in the church in North India at that time. He became a student in St John's Divinity College in Lahore, and there in close contact with a number of young men training for the ministry he was disappointed to find how low was the level of their spirituality.

He had enrolled not through any desire of his own, but out of respect and affection for Dr Lefroy, Anglican Bishop of Lahore. Dr Lefroy recognised that Sundar was unusually gifted as a preacher and that his wholehearted dedication to his Master was having its influence on others. What better than that he should be trained for the Anglican ministry, thereby opening doors for him which at present were closed? To the value of the theological training would be the added opportunity of ordination and a recognised position in the Anglican community throughout the whole of India. Deferring to the judgment of Dr Lefroy and other western missionaries who had proved themselves good friends, Sundar agreed to become a divinity student. He sat for and passed the examination given to the students after their first year in college, and still wearing his saffron robe entered the second year's course along with them.

Right from the start it was difficult for him. He was different from the other students with his distinctive appearance and unusual background. Most of them were from Christian communities and those who were not had accepted help from missionaries with the inevitable result of distancing themselves from their own people. The arrival in their midst of one who was robed like a sadhu and known to live like one caused quite a stir, and aroused a good deal of criticism and animosity on the part of some. His habit of going off for prolonged periods of private prayer mystified and irritated them. And his ardour! It wasn't natural!

One student in particular was open in his resentment, and Sundar was perplexed and dismayed at the treatment he received. Was it his own fault, he wondered? Was there something wrong with him that he was unaware of?

One day he was feeling so burdened in mind and spirit about the whole matter that he wandered off alone, sat down under a tree and started to pray. Little knowing that his persecutor had seen him and stolen up behind him, Sundar prayed aloud with tears, beseeching the Lord to show him if he himself was to blame and forgive him for anything he had done amiss. He prayed especially for the one who, unbeknown to him, was crouching behind the tree listening as he prayed God to bless him and pleaded that real love might be established between them.

His prayer was answered then and there. The eavesdropper, deeply moved by what he had heard, came forward and dropping on his knees beside Sundar asked his forgiveness. The two became fast friends, and many years later the erstwhile persecutor, by then a sincere and earnest church worker, traced his turning to Christ to the time under the tree when he heard Sundar praying for him.

It was at about this time that Stokes returned to India with three other young men to form a new brotherhood, rather on the lines of the Franciscan order. He had approached the Archbishop of Canterbury about it and having obtained that prelate's acceptance of the idea, proceeded to India, where a solemn inaugural service was held in Lahore Cathedral. There were five members of this brotherhood, one of whom was Sundar, the only Indian among them. But he took no vows. He had already made his vow alone before God, to renounce the world and devote himself to the proclamation of the gospel.

The year or so that he spent studying theology, church history, the Book of Common Prayer, apologetics and the history of religions came to an end when he learned to his amazement that once ordained he would have to limit his activities to within the Anglican community. It had never occurred to him that such restrictions would be put on him. He had already received his licence to preach but the idea of going only to Anglican congregations, and by-passing the innumerable villages where no one was proclaiming the true way of life could not be entertained. He did not come to his decision hurriedly, but the more he thought and prayed about it the more convinced he was that such a pathway was not what God had planned for him. He must be free to go to all and to have fellowship with all who loved the Lord Jesus, whatever their sect or creed. He went to Dr Lefroy, explained his position and returned his licence. The perceptive Bishop magnanimously accepted Sundar's explanation along with the licence.

Then Sundar took to the road again — a simple Christian sadhu.

For the next six or seven years Sundar moved through the towns and villages of North India, going annually to help in a holiday camp for disabled boys, occasionally staying for brief periods in a hill station or in hostels in Delhi and Simla, but always returning to what he knew to be his calling. Clad only in his saffron robe with a blanket over his shoulder he went quietly on his way, spending the early hours of each day in solitary meditation and prayer, walking mile after mile across the plains, stopping to preach wherever he thought he saw an opportunity.

His prolonged presence was not always welcome. Seeing some men reaping in a field one day, he went to them and started preaching. They listened rather indifferently for a time then began to swear at him. They did not want to hear about a strange religion, they told him. They had work to do. Then one of them picked up a stone and threw it so hard and so accurately that it cut his face. Sundar dabbed the bleeding spot and wisely said no more, but for some reason did not move away.

A short time later the man who had thrown the stone developed such a splitting headache that he had to stop work. One scythe idle at harvest time was a serious matter as Sundar knew, and without a word he went forward, picked up the scythe and started to wield it. This made a good impression on the men, especially as he went on working until they all stopped. At their invitation he went back to the village with them to have something to eat. It was not until after he had gone that they took stock of what had been reaped that day, and to their amazement found it was a greater yield than they had ever had before. Their surprise turned to awe. It was because they had had the holy man reaping with them. A holy man! But they had rejected his message. They tried to find him then but he had gone. The incident was reported in a North Indian paper by one of the reapers who wanted to hear the sadhu's message now and urged him to return to them.

On another journey, this time in the Himalayan foothills, he was met by a man who appeared to be in great distress and asked him for money. His friend, he said, had died suddenly on the road — he pointed to a figure on the ground covered with a piece of cloth — and he had no money to bury him. Sundar only had two coins and his blanket, but he gave all to the man and went on his way. A short time later the man came running after him sobbing. His friend was dead, he gasped.

Sundar naturally was mystified. 'Yes, so you told me,' he said.

'But he's really dead,' the man blurted out and then went on to admit that the whole thing had been a hoax. He and his companion had been preying on passers-by in this way for years, taking turns to feign dead and so extract money from unsuspecting travellers. But now they had lied to a holy man! They had taken his money and his blanket and this was judgment on them. His companion was already dead, the distraught man said, and now what disaster would happen to him? The man was overcome with his sense of guilt.

Sundar, of course, had the answer, telling him that there is no sin that cannot be forgiven, for God's Son, on the cross, has already borne the punishment due to the sinner. The man's heart was ready to receive what was to him astounding news, and the outcome was that after spending some time with Sundar, he went to a mission station of which Sundar told him, was duly baptised and became a church member.

Such incidents were not common, but news of

them began to get about, and when Sundar arrived in one of the cities or a hill station, there were always those who wanted to meet him. When he was in Delhi his influence on some of the students who came to his room in the hostel was transforming. One gave up an assured position in Government service to be free for full-time Christian service. Another decided to abandon all thought of secular work and train to be a pastor. More amazing than either was the high-caste student who on learning that one of the college sweepers, an 'untouchable', was ill, went to the sweepers' quarters and nursed him back to health. Such a thing had never happened in the college before.

During his periods in the hill stations or in the cities, Sundar made some friends who remained steadfast to him for the rest of his life. One of these was a young New Zealander, the Rev. T. E. Riddle, who was later to write Sundar's biography. Another was the Rev. C. F. Andrews, a professor in St Stephens College, Delhi. He first met Sundar in 1907 and noticed his youthful appearance and his shyness. While others were talking Sundar would sit quietly, apparently absorbed in his own thoughts until a question was fired at him personally when he would look up, a gleam in his deep-set, liquid brown eyes, and give a quick intelligent answer that was listened to all the more intently because of his former silence. Andrews, though an Englishman, had a deep affinity with Sundar's mystical nature, and understood him better than many of his own countrymen.

Then there was Dr E. M. Wherry, an American Presbyterian missionary who had known Sundar when he was still in his teens and had followed his career with deep interest. Dr Wherry edited a Hindustani Christian paper which came out weekly in

Ludhiana, and it was he who first launched Sundar into print, by inviting him to contribute reports of his activities for publication in his paper. Sundar, seeing in this an opportunity to inspire and challenge others with what was already becoming a dominating concern to him — the evangelisation of the peoples living in and beyond the Himalayan mountains — agreed to do so. Those reports, almost entirely concerning travels and people met on the Tibetan border, had the quite unpremeditated effect of introducing him to people who might never have heard of him. They began to be interested in this young writer and wished to see and hear him. God was preparing him for a far wider ministry than anything he had visualised for himself.

A HEART IN TUNE

God is within reach of us all, but to lay hold of him it is necessary that our hearts should be attuned to him. For us to hear the message of the wireless, which in the form of song, music or address is present in the atmosphere, it is necessary to have a receiving set which is perpetually attuned to the message. For if it were not so tuned, the existence or the non-existence of the message would be one and the same thing to us.

With and Without Christ

Chapter

6

Sundar believed in angels. However sceptical or cautious his friends from the west might be, affected as they were by the Higher Criticism of that period, he had not the slightest doubt about either the existence of these spiritual beings, or of their having come to his aid in times of danger. On his return from some of his journeys in the Himalayas he quite naturally related experiences of deliverances which he attributed to angels who appeared in the form of men. On one occasion, having been directed along a forest path that eventually led to a river, he saw that it was too wide and swift flowing for him to cross. Night was already falling, and with the sound of wild beasts in his ears he wondered how he would fare, and whether the end of his life had come. To face death alone in that isolated spot was no easier for him than for anyone else, and his eyes were filling with tears when, looking across the river he saw a man warming himself by a fire.

'Don't worry, I'm coming to help you,' the man

called out, and stepping down into the water he came across fearlessly and said to Sundar,

'Sit on my shoulders — don't be afraid.' Perched on the man's back Sundar found himself carried through the river and up the bank, thinking to himself,

'He must live near here, and so be used to crossing. I must tell him the Good News about Jesus...' On arrival at the other bank Sundar slipped off his rescuer's back, glanced around to get his bearings, then turned round to speak to him — but the man had disappeared. Neither was there any trace of the fire.

On another occasion, being unusually tired and footsore, he was trudging along in a very dejected frame of mind when he was joined by a man who walked along beside him and talked in such a friendly and uplifting manner that Sundar's mood had changed completely by the time they reached the village he was making for. But at that point, turning to his new-found friend, he found himself again alone. His companion had vanished. 'I know now that it was an angel of the Lord sent to strengthen and uphold me in my hour of weakness.'

Then there was the evening when having tried to preach in a place called Kanyan all day, only to be interrupted again and again by men who were bitterly opposed to him, he made his way out to a desert place, dropped down hungry and miserable under a tree and fell asleep. About midnight he was awakened by a touch, and a voice told him to get up and eat. There beside him were two men holding out food to eat and water to drink. Thinking they must be villagers who had taken pity on him, he took the refreshment gratefully and when he was satisfied looked up to speak to the men — but they had disappeared.

The most remarkable instance of angelic succour and deliverance that he related happened when he had reached a town in Tibet called Rasa. Here he was arrested for having entered the country to preach a foreign religion. He was brought before the head lama who passed sentence on him — a sentence which amounted to death. But the Tibetan religion forbidding them to take life, they had conceived two ways of leaving a culprit to die without actually killing him. One was to sew him up in wet yak skins, then leave him in the sun which caused the yak skins to shrink, crushing him. The other was to cast him into a dry well, cover over the top and leave him there. In either case there was no taking of life by human hands, since the forces that caused the yak skins to shrink or the body in the well to die through hunger and thirst were not under their control, so they were innocent.

The method chosen in Sundar's case was to cast him into the well. He was hustled there, the iron cover unlocked and removed, and he was pushed over the edge, down into a pit so foul that his very soul recoiled. The bottom of it was covered with dead men's bones and rotting flesh, and the stench was almost overwhelming. Then what little light had penetrated was shut out as the cover of the well was replaced and he was left in darkness.

It was far worse than anything he had ever experienced before. No one had accompanied him on this trip; he was in a country where he was unknown, and he realised that humanly speaking his situation was hopeless. There was no possibility of help from any human source, and this time the inner joy he had known in times of persecution was missing.

'My God, my God...why have you forsaken me?' The words of Jesus on the cross came to mind but without the comfort of conscious fellowship. Why, oh why had God brought him to this place of horror and left him there?

Hours passed — how many he had no means of knowing. His arm had been wrenched as he was cast into the well, but the physical pain was as nothing compared with the anguish of his soul. In relating the story years later he said he was in that well for two days and nights, and on the third night he heard a sound above. The cover of the well was being removed and then a rope was let down and a voice told him to take hold of it. Summoning what strength remained in him he slipped the noose under his arms and was slowly drawn up, to sink on the ground, conscious only that he was gulping in fresh air at last. Weak as he was from hunger and thirst, it was air his body craved more than anything. As he breathed it in he felt himself strangely revived and the pain in his wrenched arm had gone. But he was alone. There was no sign of his rescuer.

The following day, back in the village, news reached the head lama that the sadhu who had been thrown down the well was out and about again preaching. Again Sundar was brought before him. How had he escaped, the head lama demanded, but all Sundar could tell him was what had happened, and that he had seen no one. Furiously the lama asserted that someone must have stolen the key to the well, and ordered that a search be made for it. No one was more taken aback than he when it was eventually found on his own girdle.

This was very alarming. Some superior power was evidently at work, and the head lama did not like it. It was something he could not combat. He gave no further order for Sundar to be arrested, but told him to leave the district immediately. Sundar felt he had no option but to comply and left.

Sundar's reports were by no means confined to his own experiences. He frequently referred to a previously unknown martyr named Kartar Singh, about whom he had heard on one of his journeys in 1912, and whose story had greatly moved him. Sundar had left Poo and walked up the passes preaching as he went, until he came to the monastery of a celebrated lama to whom he went with the question, 'Have you in your library any book on the life of Christ?'

He then went on to explain that some years previously a Russian named Notevick claimed to have received a book from a Tibetan Buddhist library in which it stated that Jesus Christ had been to Tibet. That was not so, the lama told him. There was no such book in any of their libraries. It was true that several hundred years ago Christian preachers had arrived and converted one of their kings, but after he died his successor wiped out Christianity, and from that time on Christians had no permission to preach in Tibet.

Sundar did not report any further conversation with the head lama, but as he went from place to place in that area he encountered determined opposition and with it a threat.

'If you don't go away from here we'll treat you the same as we treated Kartar Singh.' The frequent reference to this person caused Sundar to enquire about him and this is what he learned, not only from the Tibetans but from other sources from which he was able to piece the story together.

Kartar Singh was a young Sikh from Patiala (the same area from which Sundar himself came) who had decided to become a Christian. How it came about Sundar did not know, but the reaction of his father when Kartar told him was similar to that of Sundar's own father, though even more drastic. Kartar was ordered to take off his clothes and leave them at his father's feet and go out of the home never to return. For two or three days he was almost naked, alone in the forest, but like Sundar was filled with inner peace. Then he managed to get some manual work from which he saved money to buy sufficient clothing to set out in the manner of a sadhu — to preach the gospel. And he went towards Tibet.

On the way he was baptised and spent some time diligently learning the Tibetan language before going on, preaching as he went, until he arrived at the town of Tashigang. There he remained for three months preaching to any who would listen. But opposition increased — on one occasion he was forcibly ejected from the town, only to return saying that he would not leave the place whatever they did to him, for he was willing to die to bring them the truth about his Lord and what he had done that they might receive eternal salvation.

Then he was brought before the head lama and sentence was passed on him. The lama instructed that he was to be taken up a hill and there sewn into wet yak skins and left in the sun. As he was taken up he said, 'I shall not come down again — but I shall rise to heaven to be with my dear Lord.' Having sewn him into the wet yak skins the executioners left him, but returned from time to time to see what effect it was having on him, and were amazed and puzzled when they found him singing and praying. 'The spirit of one of the gods must be in him,' some of them said. For three days they came and at last they saw him die — praying the Lord to receive his spirit and to forgive his enemies.

Again and again with glowing face, Sundar told the story of Kartar Singh. And there was a sequel to it. One day in Patiala station, he was relating this story when he saw an old man on the outskirts of the crowd weeping. On enquiry he learned that the old man was Kartar Singh's father. Seeking him out, Sundar talked very earnestly to him, with the result that the old man became a Christian though he never had the courage to confess Christ openly.

Nor was that the only outcome of the life and death of Kartar Singh. The chief secretary of the lama who had sentenced him obtained possession of Kartar's New Testament, and with the memory of Kartar's death still fresh in his mind read it — and reading, was convinced of its truth, to the extent that not only did he put his trust in Jesus Christ, but told the lama he had done so. The lama was furiously angry and passed on him the same sentence as on Kartar. In this case however, he was not left in the yak skins long enough to die. He was cruelly tormented with red hot skewers thrust into his body, then dragged through the streets by a rope tied around his body and eventually thrown on a dust heap outside the town and left to die. But he did not die. Gradually he recovered enough strength to crawl away, and recovering from his awful ordeal returned to the town where people were so over-awed at seeing him alive and strong that they dared do nothing further to oppose him. It was from him that Sundar learned about the witness and death of Kartar.

Even stranger perhaps than the story of Kartar Singh, was that which Sundar told about the Maharishi of Kailash. This extraordinary man, who claimed to be 300 years old, lived as a hermit in the Kailash range, a remote though beautiful area in which it was known that a number of Buddhist and other hermits lived. Most of them were there, isolated even from each other, and existing in the utmost austerity in the pursuit of the peace which ultimately meant final oblivion. But the Maharishi was quite different. He was a Christian, and Sundar came on him one day quite by accident.

He was scrambling along an entirely unknown path when he stumbled, slid down the side of the mountain, and found himself at the mouth of a cave in which sat the strangest creature he had ever seen. It was an old man, with hair sprouting not only on face and chin but apparently all over his body. He looked kindly but without surprise at Sundar, and entered into conversation with him freely, explaining where he came from and why he was there.

He was born in Alexandria in Egypt, he said, and had been baptised by the nephew of St Francis Xavier. He had travelled in many countries preaching the gospel and could speak over twenty languages. The time came, however, when he realised that he was too old for that sort of life, so he had come to this remote spot to devote himself to prayer. It was evident from what he told Sundar that he had a supernatural knowledge of some of Sundar's own friends. One example was of a missionary he knew, of whom the Maharishi said,

'Tell him that I cannot pray for him while he continues in that secret sin. If I pray for him that sin will prevent the answer.' Sundar was surprised, having no idea that the missionary had a secret sin, but when eventually he met him he passed on the Maharishi's message and the man, with tears of contrition, acknowledged a sin which no one else could have known of.

Another example was that of the four men who some time later actually set out with Sundar to visit the Maharishi, but found the journey beyond their strength and turned back. When Sundar himself arrived the Maharishi said,

'Now tell me, Sundar, how you happened to come? The others have gone back,' and he mentioned accurately the names of all four of them. Then he said he would pray for them and added, 'Tell them to give up the desire of getting higher pay and keep on doing the Lord's work.'

The Maharishi also told Sundar of a sort of secret society in India, which he called the Secret Sanyasi Mission, with a history going back to the time of Christ. There were now about 24,000 members of the mission, the Maharishi said, but they remained secret believers. Sundar was not altogether surprised at this for in the course of his travels he had been unobtrusively helped by people who told him they belonged to this mission. But they were not yet prepared to come out into the open.

All this, and things of a more mystical nature, concerning angels and saints and the spirits of departed Christians, the Maharishi told Sundar who related some of them later, thereby arousing considerable discussion and speculation on the part of those who questioned the veracity of his reports, and implied that the Maharishi himself was a figment of Sundar's imagination. He was not unduly concerned — let people think what they would. He did not want to enter into arguments, nor a lot of unnecessary correspondence either. His main task he still saw as travelling around proclaiming the gospel of Jesus Christ, and this he continued to do — but not without inner conflict.

There were times when he was tempted to give up the life of a sadhu, marry and settle down like other men. Could he not live a sincere Christian life in a normal way, and still devote himself to preaching? Others did so. Yet even deeper than his natural instinct was the fervent desire to know his Master better, and follow him all the way. He remembered how Jesus, at the very commencement of his ministry, went into the wilderness and fasted for forty days and forty nights. The thought remained in his mind, and he felt that he, too, should fast for that period. He knew where he could go to do it — south of Dehra Dun was a forest in which was an area so thickly overgrown that only the bamboo cutters penetrated it. There, far from human habitations, he could be alone with God, asking for blessing on what he had already done, an empowering for future service, and seeking to live on a higher plane in the spiritual life.

Travelling by train towards Dehra Dun he met a Roman Catholic doctor, to whom he confided his intention. The doctor tried to dissuade him from attempting such a fast. It would kill him, he said. Sundar remained firm in his resolve, so the doctor asked for the names and addresses of some of his friends, so that if anything happened he could let them know. To this Sundar acceded.

Then he went on, towards the forest. He took with him his New Testament and forty stones. The doctor had told him the likely effects of going without food and drink for a prolonged period, and he had decided that the best way of keeping track of time would be to throw away one stone each day. And so he started on his vigil deep in the forest, alone.

The first days were physically hard. Hunger brought on a burning pain in his stomach which became quite acute, but it eased off after a time, and he merely became increasingly weak — so weak, in fact, that he stopped putting aside a stone each day. He could not even turn himself. At one stage he sensed rather than saw, a lion or some other wild beast, and heard a roar, but could not tell how near it was. But with the dimming of physical sensibilities there came an increasing awareness of the spiritual world, of the presence of God. The deep joy and inner peace he had known since his turning to Christ were increased — he had no desire to end his fast. Then there was granted to him, as weakness and exhaustion took their toll of his body, a fresh vision of Christ.

It was different from the appearance on that never-to-be-forgotten night when he had seen with his own eyes the risen Lord Jesus. This time it was the Man on the Throne in his glory that was revealed to him, his face radiant, the wounds in his hands and feet clearly visible, but somehow beautified. It was inexpressible. Yet with it came to Sundar the conviction that there was still work for him to do, and that he would be preserved alive to do it. Then he lapsed into unconsciousness.

WORK AND PRAYER

Prayer without work is as bad as work without prayer. As a clucking hen to satisfy its instinct continues to sit in some dark corner even after its eggs have been removed, so the life of those who remove themselves from the busy life of the world and spend their time wholly in prayer is as fruitless as is the hen's.

With and Without Christ

7

Bishop Lefroy, now the Metropolitan of India, looked sadly at the telegram he had just received. 'Sundar Singh asleep in Christ,' it read. The bishop had received a letter from Sundar a few weeks previously, in which he had mentioned he was feeling ill, and was going to stay with a friend. Since then he had heard nothing until this telegram arrived. Then he learned that the Rev. J. Redman in Simla, Dr E. M. Wherry in Ludhiana, Canon Wigram in Lahore and two other clergymen had received the same message. None of them knew the sender of the telegram, which was merely signed 'Smith', but none of them had any reason to doubt that it was genuine. Enquiries made at the place from which it had been sent had elicited the information that it had been handed in by 'a gentleman in a black coat'. In the sort of life Sundar had been living, anything could happen.

So the young sadhu was dead! The sense of loss throughout the missionary community, as well as the churches where Sundar was known, was deep. He had in no way conformed to the usual pattern for converts in India, but they could not fail to see that his unique manner of life, and presentation of the word of God, was having a profound influence in the churches. And as a person he had endeared himself to them. Glowing reports of his short life and witness were published, testimonies too, to his personality and character. One Anglican Canon wrote:

'He was a perfect gentleman, refined and cultured in his manners, gentle and courteous, simple and unaffected. He had scarcely a loud enough voice for bazaar preaching, but this method did not seem to appeal to him. He would rather sit and discuss religion with a small group around him. His method was to preach for as many days as he felt called, being lodged and fed by Christian friends; he then went on to the next stage when they gave him the train fare. Had he lived he would have been a power among his own people. May many more be raised up like Sundar Singh.'

In Simla, in the Church of St Thomas, a memorial service was held, and a fund opened for the erection of a tablet in his memory.

Then came surprising news. The Rev. J. Redman received a postcard from Canon Wigram in which he said:

'Have you heard that Sundar Singh is alive after all? The Bishop of Calcutta has just sent me a letter of his written from Annfield, 21 February.'

Sundar himself, of course, knew nothing of all this. Two bamboo cutters stumbling through the forest had come upon his weak and emaciated body, and seeing he was a sadhu, and still breathing, had carried him to some people who put him on the train to Dehra Dun. Here, providentially, two or three Christians from the village of Annfield saw him, and although he was so altered in appearance that they did not recognise him, they knew who he was by the name in his New Testament. Placing him gently on their bullock cart, they conveyed him to the home of their pastor. Here, for over a week, he was given only liquids until he was strong enough to digest a little food.

He recovered slowly, though steadily, but he had a very hazy appreciation of time, and the duration of the fast. A fortnight after being brought to Annfield he wrote:

'As directed by God I kept a fast of forty days, from which I derived much spiritual benefit. Exactly on the fortieth day, by God's plan a few men came to the forest to cut bamboos and brought me from there. I had become very weak, but now I am able to walk again a little.' Actually, all the evidence produced later went to prove that the fast only lasted about half that time, and his inaccuracy in his references to it was to provide his enemies with a lever to be used against him in later years. But from his point of view at the time, he had entered on a forty day fast in what he believed was God's purpose for him, and therefore it had been fulfilled.

When he had recovered sufficiently he set off again, making towards the Himalayas. Not until he reached Simla did he hear about the telegrams that had been received. The only explanation he could give was that the doctor he had consulted before his fast must have assumed he had died, and sent them. The whole affair had resulted in publicity which focussed more attention on him than ever. He had already become well known and quite in demand as a speaker at Christian gatherings. The report of his death, followed by his reappearance, naturally increased curiosity, making him a distinctive figure, one who stood out rather like a prophet of old. It was all rather embarrassing.

Such was the outward result of his fast. Inwardly it

had been one of the most significant events in his spiritual life, of which the full effects were only apparent to him later. But even during the fast itself he had gained an understanding of things that previously had perplexed him. He had sometimes wondered if the peace and joy he experienced was from what he called 'a hidden power in his own life' — a hangover from the Pantheism that regards God as identical with the forces of nature. As he lay alone in the forest, becoming weaker and weaker each day, the peace so far from diminishing increased. This convinced him that it was a heaven-born peace which had nothing to do with his natural faculties.

It was the same with regard to his spirit. What would be the effect of death on his spirit? But he realised that as his physical and mental faculties were decreasing, his spiritual powers were more alert and active. As he described it later,

'The brain is only the office where the spirit works. Or, to change the analogy, the brain is like an organ on which the organist plays. Two or three notes may go wrong and produce no music — but that does not imply the absence of the organist!'

Perhaps what impressed him even more than the solving of those metaphysical questions was the permanent influence the fast had on his character. The temptation to give up the sadhu manner of life and return to a more normal way of living had lost its power almost to the extent of being non-existent.

'I saw that though it is no sin for others to live in comfort and have money and home, God's call to me was different.'

A rebellious spirit had been dealt with, too. There were times before the fast when he had complained inwardly at being hungry and thirsty. 'Why doesn't the Lord provide? Why did he tell me not to take money with me? If I had money I could buy what I needed, and I need food!' But after the fast, when facing some physical hardship, he found himself thinking:

'It is my Father's will,' and accepting it without murmuring. In some inexplicable way he found himself living on a higher plane. Even his irritability was subdued. This irritability revealed itself when he was tired, and people came and asked him a lot of questions. He was painfully conscious of it, tried to hide it, but although it was still there even after the fast, it was there in a much lesser degree.

Sundar's arrival in Simla was noted by his friend the New Zealander, T. E. Riddle in his diary, '16 March, 1913. Sundar Singh arrived again. Going now to the Tibet border.' The compelling urge to go to the mountains never seemed to leave him, and he planned his preaching tours in the thickly populated plains so that he was free to go up the passes when the snows melted. For the next fourteen months he continued his usual programme of travelling and preaching, until by the end of May 1914, he was on the border of Nepal.

It was not easy to enter that Hindu kingdom without a passport, and for a Christian it was impossible to obtain one. Sundar was twice turned away by border guards before he managed to get in. Once inside he was encouraged by the reception he received at the villages he passed through. He confined himself mainly to reading aloud from the Nepali New Testament, for although he understood the language he could not speak it fluently, and found conversation difficult. But the villages were in very mountainous territory, and as he wrote later,

'...the roads are awful. One is tired by ascents and

descents and the crossing of streams. The 7th of June will always be in my memory — the fatigue of the journey, the extreme hunger and thirst, the heavy showers of rain, the long ascent. A terrible blast of wind threw me into a cave.

'O praised be the Lord! Though I fell from such a height I did not get any hurt at all... Then the different stages of the crucifixion of Jesus came before me in a vision.

'First, he was awake in the garden of Gethsemane all night.

'Secondly, he was hungry and thirsty.

'Thirdly, due to the lashes and the crown of thorns he was bleeding.

'Fourthly, besides all these troubles he had to lift up the cross himself. For these reasons he fell down when he was climbing Golgotha...

'O dear Lord, my cross is nothing before Thine...'

But his own sufferings were not yet over in Nepal.

The next day he reached Ilam, a garrison town, and found the bazaar full of people. He took up his stand in front of the post office and started to preach, the New Testament is his hand. Quite a large crowd gathered, and when he offered Gospels to any who could read there were those who came forward to receive them. At this point there was an interruption. An official arrived and angrily demanded to know who had given him permission to enter Nepal and preach a foreign religion.

Sundar replied that he had come at the command of the Officer of all officers, the Raja of all Rajas — the Creator.

'Why?' snapped the official.

'Christ has called all nations to receive eternal life, and Nepal must hear this good news, too.'

The official did not want to discuss the matter. He

was all for putting Sundar in jail for six months, the prescribed penalty for illegal entry, there and then. However, another official pointed out that if this preacher were put in jail he might persuade some of the other prisoners to become Christians. So it was decided that a different form of punishment should be inflicted.

'They seized me and threw me into prison. They took off my clothes and fastened my hands and feet in a block of wood, and bringing a lot of leeches left them near me...For two or three hours I felt my sufferings very much indeed, but afterwards my Lord by his holy presence turned my prison into a paradise...

'When I was singing, full of joy, many people came to the door to listen, and I again began to preach. Then they released me.'

They probably thought he was mad.

'To such an extent had the leeches sucked my blood that on the following day I suffered dizziness as I walked.' Then he added,

'Glory to God that he honoured me by letting me suffer for his name.'

He was a strong man. He walked the thirty miles back to Darjeeling within two days, and wrote to the Rev. J. Redman in Simla telling of the conversation with the Nepali officer, but not mentioning his brief imprisonment. He did not want to create another sensation among his friends. Nor did he want the incident to reach the ears of those in the Government who might start enquiries as to why a British subject had received such treatment.

Perhaps there was another reason of which he himself was only dimly aware — the instinctive shutting of the door of memory on a particularly traumatic experience until over-strung emotions had been quietened. At any rate, when he arrived at the home of his friend Tharchin, who saw the leech marks on his back and applied iodine to them, Sundar gave no explanation of how he got them, and a few days later the two of them set out for the little country of Sikkim.

Sundar had first met Tharchin in Poo, where he was employed by the Moravian missionaries. Tharchin was of Tibetan stock, and willingly accompanied Sundar on the journey they both hoped would bring them into Tibet. They arrived in Gangtok the capital of Sikkim, but there they could go no further without official permission. For a whole week they waited there, Sundar going daily to the police station to enquire if the necessary permit had come. After eight days of futile waiting he said:

'Perhaps it is not God's will that we should go any further. We'd better go back.' So they returned to India, and Sundar slowly made his way back to Sabathu, near the hill station of Kotgarh, where Stokes had established a school for boys.

It was here when he was alone in the woods one day, praying for the boys, that he was given what he often referred to as 'the gift of ecstasy'.

He had had strange spiritual experiences before — experiences that were quite distinct from the revelations he had had of the Lord Jesus Christ but which were, nevertheless, of a spiritual nature. He had heard voices and music, seen lights. As he explained years later:

'Sometimes it was as if there were sharp needles pricking me, and I saw light, but not real light. I think there is something in the heart which enables one instinctively to judge whether such experiences are of God or not...Sometimes I felt a sort of heat, but there was no joy in it, and I found these experiences were a hindrance...I recognised that they were not real. The fort, that is the heart, was not reached by them.

92

'Sometimes Satan merely whispered, sometimes his words were clear. Sometimes he said, "You are wrong, this is not the way"; "You have left truth behind"; "You are a sinner, you cannot be saved." When I listened to the voices I felt troubled. When I prayed to the Lord to help me everything stopped, the heat, the whisperings, the shiverings and the prickings. Then I said, "These things are from Satan."'

His personal experiences put him in a good position to sound a note of warning in the years that lay ahead.

'Mystics should be very careful about these things, especially beginners. Those who have been living in the world very naturally think that these experiences are great things because they have seen nothing like them before, but they come from Satan or other beings of the lower spirit world.

'These spirits know something of the future but not a great deal. Just as in India we can prophesy what the weather will be like for some weeks ahead, so the lower spirits, through their superior knowledge of the tendency of things, can prophesy events a short time ahead, and this helps them in deceiving men. Prophets inspired by God can prophesy many many years ahead. That is the difference.

'It is these spirits of the lower spirit world with which spiritualists get into contact. From them spiritualists get interesting things, but they are ultimately deceived by the spirits, who begin by giving them ninety-nine things that are true and one that is false, and gradually increase the proportion of false and decrease the true until they lead people on to atheism or some other false position. The truly spiritual man has that within him which feels an instinctive antipathy to the kind of things which are told him by spirits of the lower world. If we seek only what is interesting,

93

we shall never reach as far as the real higher spirit world.'

Aware as he was of spiritual forces, both divine and demonic, he was quite unprepared for what happened up there in the woods, praying alone.

Suddenly it was as though his spiritual eyes were opened, and he saw the glories of the Kingdom of God. Jacob in his dream saw angels ascending from earth to God in heaven, and descending again to where he lay sleeping. Sundar saw more than that. It was as though the words of Hebrews 12:22-24 became a living reality:

'You have come to Mount Zion, to the heavenly Jerusalem, the city of the living God.

'You have come to thousands upon thousands of angels in joyful assembly, to the church of the first-born, whose names are written in heaven.

'You have come to God, the judge of all men, to the spirits of righteous men made perfect, to Jesus the mediator of a new covenant, and to the sprinkled blood that speaks a better word than the blood of Abel.'

What he saw was beyond description, but he did the best he could years later, when talking to close friends of what he termed his ecstasies:

'In that world there are many things which correspond to things of beauty in this world, mountains, trees and flowers, but with all imperfections taken away. The mountains, trees and flowers of this earth are only the shadow of what I see there. Everything there, even inanimate objects, are so made that they continually give praise, and all quite spontaneously.

'Christ on his throne is always in the centre, a figure ineffable and indescribable. The face, as I see it in ecstasy, with my spiritual eyes, is very much the same as I saw it at my conversion with my bodily eyes. He has scars with blood flowing from them. The scars are not ugly, but glowing and beautiful. He has a beard on his face. The long hair of his head is like gold, like glowing light. His face is like the sun, but its light does not dazzle me. It is a sweet face, always smiling — a loving glorious smile. Christ is not terrifying at all.

'And all around the throne of Christ, extending to infinite distances, are multitudes of glorious spiritual beings. Some of them are saints, some of them angels. These are indistinguishable. "The difference is not important. We are all one here," they told me. They all look like younger brothers of Christ. They are all glorified, but his glory is far more glorious than their glory, and they differ among themselves in degree of glory, something like a difference of colour...

'Their clothes are, as it were, made of light, not dazzling but many-coloured. (There are more colours there than in this world. There is nothing here so beautiful, not even diamonds and precious stones.) When they speak to me they put their thoughts into my heart in a single moment...I did not have to learn the language of the spiritual world...When we leave the body and enter that world, we speak it as easily and naturally as a new-born babe breathes the moment it enters this world, though it has not done such a thing before.'

'In these visions we have most wonderful talks. This is the real communion of saints, which is spoken of in the Apostles' Creed. We talk about spiritual things, and problems which no one here can solve. This good company solves them easily. There are very many things which I can see and hear there and of which I have a clear picture in my mind, but I can't express them even in Hindustani, much less in English, and some of them are things that it would be no

95

use even trying to express, because their beauty would be lost if they could be taken out of that world and put into this...'

As well one might expect a grub at the bottom of a pond to understand the ecstasy of the dragon-fly darting in the sunlight over the glinting waters amid the fragrance of the air and the songs of birds! Sundar could appreciate the reticence of Paul when writing of the third heaven (2 Corinthians 12:1-6).

'St Paul was afraid people would misunderstand his meaning; and that is why he spoke of the experience as if it had been not his own but somebody else's, saying "I know a man in Christ who..."'

'This was because he knew that, if he spoke of the visions as his own, people would have come and bothered him by asking foolish questions, and would have misunderstood the answers he had given them.'

Then Sundar added feelingly, 'He was very wise not to try and tell them!'

This gift of ecstasy, as he called it, this transporting of the spirit into the unseen heavenly realm, was to him like going home. With other men whose duties took them far afield, the return to their own abode provided them with the rest and refreshment they found nowhere else. Sundar had no such place of refuge. But when, as happened from time to time after that first experience, he suddenly found himself in heaven, all tension was relieved. There was no sense of strangeness — he felt perfectly at home. And he always emerged back into normal, often wearisome human life, refreshed and invigorated. As he told his friends,

'During the years of my life as a sadhu there have been many times when suffering from hunger, thirst or persecution, I might have been tempted to give it up, but for the gift of these times of ecstasy...

'But these I would not give up for the whole world.'

REDEEM THE TIME

We ought to make the best possible use of God-given opportunities, and should not waste our precious time by our neglect or carelessness. Many people say, 'there is plenty of time to do this or that; don't worry!' But they do not realise that if they do not make good use of this short time, the habit formed now will be so ingrained that when more time is given to us this habit will become our second nature and we shall waste that time also.

With and Without Christ

8

'My dear son, light of my eyes, comfort of my life, may you live long!'

So began the letter which Sundar received from his father one summer day in 1916. If he had a momentary hope that it would continue in the same affectionate vein he was speedily disillusioned. After that primary warm greeting, the tone of it changed promptly. His father wanted to know why he had not replied to the message sent to him through the tailor Dasundhu? This had presumably been in the nature of a command to agree to a suitable marriage. The letter continued:

'I do not ask for your opinion. I order you to marry soon. Does the Christian religion teach you to disobey your parents?' Could he not serve his Guru Christ as a married man? Did he intend to efface the name of the family? And what about the home and the property?

Following these arguments his father came out with what appeared to be a tempting offer. If Sundar would agree to the proposed betrothal, he would immediately be in receipt of a monthly sum of 300 rupees. But if not…'Whatever stands in your name, don't hope for it!'

In his reply Sundar pointed out that he had already given up any expectation of receiving money or property when he became a Christian, and that having put his hand to the plough he was not prepared to look back. As for the matter of marriage,

'I am always obedient to you and ready to serve you heart and soul, but I cannot marry because besides you I have my Heavenly Father, whom I must serve with all my mind and might. This is the ideal of my life. If I marry I will not be able to do my duty faithfully.' Then he added the significant words,

'Furthermore, I have no desire for marriage.'

The subject of marriage was often being brought up to him at that time, not only by his father, but by others. Well-meaning people wrote to him or spoke to him about it, and he confided to a friend of his how trying he found it. Eventually his friend, with his permission, wrote to the weekly paper edited by Dr Wherry, explaining that as a fellow countryman Sundar Singh often consulted him about difficult matters, and continued,

'In regard to marriage I found him absolutely disgusted. I came to know that he will never, never marry, not because he thinks the pure relation of matrimony bad, but because he takes it to be a great hindrance in the service which God has entrusted to him.

'I respectfully request that Christian lady who wants to marry him…those gentlemen who every now and then, by letter or orally, press Sundar Singh to marry, are respectfully requested in future not to do so. Instead of this they should help him with their prayers. From his conversation it is clear that he thinks these letters in which there is mention of marriage, and those people who advise him to marry, are a hard trial to him.'

There were times when Sundar wondered why God allowed it. Then the thought came to him, 'This is perhaps also to my benefit that God allows such a trial to come so that my youth may be fully examined, whether I have placed it solely at the feet of God, and so that, Oh God, thou mayest use it as *thou* wishest.'

Marriage was not the only matter that was constantly being broached at that time, distracting his attention from what he saw as his primary calling — preaching. What he had written and told about the mysterious hermit in the Kailash range, the Maharishi, was stirring curiosity and speculation. He received a number of letters enquiring about the Maharishi, many of them casting doubt on the very existence of such a being. The young sadhu, they implied, had imagined the whole thing as the result of a dream, or a wandering mind in his times of meditation.

Again through the pages of Dr Wherry's newspaper, Sundar did his best to deal with the matter, explaining that he was too deeply involved in his work for God to reply individually to all the letters,

'So I hope that the respectable objectors will excuse me if I quickly tell them through this newspaper a few things.' Rather tartly he continued,

'As I have previously written, some of my friends think that this is only a dream or a spiritual meditation in which an old man came and talked, but that in reality there is no such man. Well...if people think that it is true and believe it, our salvation does not depend on it, and if they do not believe it, there is no loss, for our salvation is from God who at every time and everywhere is with us. I do not like knocking heads together like rams. Say whatever you like. Your

101

servant will listen to it silently and will continue praying for your welfare.' Then he outlined briefly his first meeting with the Maharishi, and offered to escort any who were prepared to make the journey to see him for themselves.

It was as a result of this offer that those four men, Indians and Anglo-Indians, set out with him in the Spring of 1917. He had warned them that it would be hard travelling with streams to be crossed and hardships and difficulties of many kinds to be faced. Two days of walking were sufficient for one of them, and he decided to give it up. Ten days after setting out together from Dehra Dun the last of them left him, and he continued his journey alone.

His chosen route this time was through Almora, where he met a Sikh now working in connection with the London Missionary Society. Yanus Singh had also travelled in Tibet, and was writing a book about it. He produced a map and asked Sundar to point out the places to which he had gone. Together they traced the routes, and as Sundar mentioned the names of villages and towns he had visited Yanus Singh nodded — he knew those places, too.

A few days after this pleasant interlude Sundar, pressing on again towards Tibet, became suddenly feverish, and so weakened he was unable to walk. A bitterly cold wind was blowing, but there was nowhere to take shelter. He was alone, and he knew there was a precipitous ascent of some seven miles ahead of him.

It was a case of 'climb — or die'. Standing there he prayed earnestly for the strength he needed, then, without waiting for any conscious empowering,

'I began to ascend the hill.' The step of faith had an unexpected result. 'This exertion caused so much perspiration that all my clothes became wet. When I reached my destination, I found that I was all right. The fever had left me when I perspired profusely. Had I lain down on a bed and begun to take medicines, God knows for how long the fever would have troubled me.'

Further on, he came to a village where a big fair was in progress, at the centre of which a buffalo was being cruelly tortured. Men with sharp knives cut at it, then filled the wounds with powdered red chillies. The poor creature, maddened with pain ran to and fro, its tongue hanging out.

'But those cruel people seemed to rejoice over it. They thought their sins would be forgiven by doing so. When the buffalo fell down on the ground exhausted, the people beat him to death with sticks, and his blood was offered to their deity.'

And Sundar thought of Christ...

So had Christ suffered at the hands of man...

'When I saw this I had the image of our Lord Christ before my eyes. It is not by means of the blood of goats and calves, but by the blood of the only Son of God, that we obtain salvation.' Then he added simply,

'I had very good opportunities for preaching the Bible to the people at this fair.'

He was not so successful with the half-wild tribe called the Raots, living in the forest of Askot, about twenty miles from Almora.

'I went to these people, preaching the Holy Bible en route. These people look wild, even in their appearance. They wear only a small piece of cloth round the waist. Some of them have improved and have begun to wear clothes, but further on in the denser jungle you will come across strange things. I was walking alone when I saw a man and a woman and their four children coming out of a cave and running very fast, faster than a horse. They had long hair on their bodies, and their complexions were dark. They were all quite naked. They were afraid to come near a habitation and lived miles away from villages.' They had run away when they saw him, and others were obviously afraid of him.

'I had a mind to stop among these wild human beings for a few days, but as they were afraid to come near me, my further stay there was useless.' So he went on again, towards Mount Kailash.

This was to be his third visit to the Maharishi living there, and in his contribution to Dr Wherry's weekly periodical, dated 13 July 1917, he made special mention of the position of the mountain and its characteristics. He wrote so clearly that it was evidently no figment of his own imagination.

'Mount Kailash is situated in Western Tibet. Some may think that this Kailash is the one near Chini where there is a hospital maintained by the Salvation Army. I may let you know that the real Kailash is as far from Chini as from Dehra Dun, that is to say about 300 miles...The highest peak of Kailash, which is 21,850 feet above sea level, always remains covered with snow. Nature has made this peak in the form of a temple having a cross thereon. It is a very beautiful place. That is the reason why it was selected by the Rishis for the purpose of prayer. The people of India and Tibet consider Kailash as the abode of the gods, and call it Paradise...

'The ways of God are very inscrutable. Although the place is so very cold, there are several springs of hot water close by. Some people would think it impossible that there could exist springs of hot water in such a place. In the same way some people would think it impossible that the Maharishi could remain in such a cold place in winter. But the fact is, the springs of hot water and the Maharishi are there, and if a

104

person does not believe he had better go and see for himself...

'Kailash is about a week's journey from Pithoragarh. It may be a month's journey for others but it is only a week's journey for me, because I can easily walk one hundred miles in three days. Pithoragarh lies at a distance of about sixty-three miles from the nearest railway station.'

Then he threw down a challenge, which he was evidently prepared to see accepted.

'Adventurous people have travelled to the North Pole and the South; it is therefore not difficult for such people to visit Kailash.'

A fortnight later he contributed another instalment to Dr Wherry's paper. In it he related how he had met a Tibetan lama who was performing a pilgrimage to Kailash, and whom he had taken to see the Maharishi.

'We walked by the east of Kailash via Gorikond and after crossing a stream ascended a hill...While walking in the snow we saw some wonderful scenery, but our lips became stiff on account of the intense cold and we could not speak a single word.

'On the evening of the following day we reached our destination. We found the Maharishi reading a very old manuscript in Greek, bound in leather...We both salaamed him respectfully and sat down.' Then conversation began.

It started with the Maharishi reading three chapters from St John's Gospel. Then the lama asked him,

'Are you not Lama Nausang who disappeared?...A great row has now begun in your temple. Will you not go back and give the people the necessary instructions?'

The Maharishi replied that the Lama Nausang was dead, and that he himself had nothing to do with the temple. He was just a humble servant of the Lord Christ, spending his time in prayer.

'It is not my business to stop quarrels. This world is a world of strife. These disputes will not cease until Satan, who is at the root of all these quarrels, is seized and imprisoned. The time is now drawing near when Satan shall be hurled down headlong in the bottomless pit of perdition.' Then Sundar went on to report more of what the Maharishi told them, much of which he had heard and related after his first visit. What he wrote and told about the Christian hermit only served to create more curiosity about this strange person, and Sundar was constantly assailed by people coming to ask questions about him. Eventually Sundar ceased to respond to these interrogations.

'My mission in the world is to preach Christ, not the Maharishi,' he said.

'My mission in the world.' He was to discover that his mission in the world would lead him far wider afield than anything he had imagined or thought of for himself. Until now his activities had been confined to North India and the mountainous regions bordering the vast Himalayan range. He was in a place called Baroda one evening at the end of 1917, and he had arranged to leave on the five o'clock train next morning to return to Sabathu when his plans were suddenly changed. It happened when he was in a state of ecstasy. The instruction was given to him to go to South India. It was quite unexpected, but he had no doubt that it was a divine directive, and without hesitation he went and told his host that he would not be catching the five o'clock train next morning, after all.

A few hours later he received a telegram, urging him to come to South India.

Unknown to him, his reputation had gone before him. Not only through Dr Wherry's paper, but through what had been written about him by an ardent admirer of his who was warden of a hostel for students in Agra, his name was becoming known. Doors had opened slowly and rather grudgingly for him in the north. In the south they opened wide and promptly. He found himself ushered into a new chapter of his life, in which adulation and popularity were to test the reality of his discipleship to the One who humbled himself.

GROWTH THROUGH PAIN

Diamonds do not dazzle with beauty unless they are cut. When cut, the rays of the sun fall on them and make them shine with wonderful colours. So when we are cut into shape by the cross we shall shine as jewels in the Kingdom of God.

In Switzerland a shepherd broke the leg of a sheep. When asked why he had done so, he said that she had the bad habit of leading other sheep astray and taking them to dangerous heights and precipices. The sheep was so angry that when the shepherd came to feed her she sometimes tried to bite him. But after a time she became friendly and would lick his hands. Just so, through sorrow and suffering, God leads those who have been disobedient and rebellious to the path of safety and eternal life.

Reality and Religion

Chapter

9

There was little enough to distinguish Vincent David from the other students in the college in Poona beyond the fact that he was very proficient in Hindustani. This familiarity with the language spoken by the Christian sadhu from the north, Sundar Singh, and Vincent's own evident Christian faith, combined to make him the choice when it came to appointing an interpreter. The sadhu could not speak the languages common to South India, and his knowledge of English was limited, so that speaking even to an educated audience would have been difficult. There was such a widespread curiosity about him in the churches around Poona that to meet all the demands to hear as well as to see him, an interpreter was needed.

So Vincent David found himself in the rather awe-inspiring position of accompanying the sadhu and interpreting for him at what were often very big meetings. It also gave him the opportunity of seeing the sadhu in a variety of situations, in private as well as in public. Wherever he went people hung around, hoping to speak to him, or at least to have the chance of a smile or a handshake. More than thirty years later, when Vincent David was a leading layman in the Diocese of Bombay, the memories of those days were clear and vivid. They made a lasting impression on him.

The sadhu's very appearance was distinctive. In the south of India, where Christianity, if weak, was deeply entrenched, with its roots going back by tradition to the first century AD, and with nearly two hundred years of Protestant missionary work recently added to it, pictures of Christ were not uncommon, and they all had similar characteristics. When the tall, well-built, bearded sadhu, clad only in his long saffron robe with a shawl over his shoulder stepped from a train or entered a room, there would sometimes be a sudden, short hush before the people who were waiting for him started talking again. They all knew what it was. He reminded them of Jesus Christ.

It was not only his garment, for there were others to be seen from time to time in the saffron robe of the sadhu. Some of them were unkempt and dirty, and there was that about them that made children shrink away. But children did not shrink away from this sadhu. They were drawn to him, and schoolboys flocked to hear him wherever they knew he would be preaching, as well as older people.

'One feels it is not his personal attraction that draws people, but the simplicity and sincerity of his life. The Indians are much impressed by his quiet life of prayer and asceticism,' reported a Sister of the Society of St John the Evangelist, adding that the people idolised him.

One of the fathers of the Society, who invited him to tea, took him to task on this point. He admired the great work he was doing for Christ, the Father said, but why did he allow himself to be called 'sadhu' or 'saint'?

'I don't want people to call me sadhu,' was the reply. 'I shall be quite happy if they merely call me Sundar Singh. But because I am leading a different kind of life from others, they call me sadhu out of their love for me. Sadhu does not mean "saint". Sadhu simply means one who follows a Sadhana, that is, a method of prayer and devotion.'

The Father was still not quite satisfied. 'When the Lord Jesus Christ was addressed as "Good Master" even he said "Call no man good, only God," ' he persisted. The sadhu had an answer ready for that too.

'The same Lord Jesus commanded, "Call no man in this world Father. You have only one Father, who is in heaven," ' he said, adding gently,

'Yet out of respect for you we call you "Father", and you also accept the title...'

The conversation, if frank, was quite friendly, and the sadhu was taken round to see the work being done by the Society. He said little, but asked intelligent questions, and showed his appreciation of everything, especially the care being taken of the babies in the crêche. Nowhere else had he seen babies being so lovingly tended, he said, and remarked to Vincent,

'We do not know what these little children are thinking about, but they look straight up to God — and their upward glance is an act of thanksgiving.' He adapted reverently to the customs of his host, genuflecting in the Chapel of the Reserved Sacrament, then raising his arms in prayer 'that his church shall stand until the Second Coming.' He spoke out sternly against half-heartedness and hypocrisy, but always with respect when he encountered sincerity, even when it was among the adherents of Hinduism.

The few days Vincent spent with the sadhu were

challenging and inspiring, but when the time came for Sundar to move on he returned to college, expecting to settle in again to his course of study. He was quite unprepared for what happened a day or two later. It was on Friday, and he was attending a history lecture when someone came in with a telegram for him. He read it with amazement. It was from the sadhu, requesting him to proceed immediately to Kolhapur to join him there. An interpreter was needed.

Vincent's heart leapt. An interpreter was needed, and the sadhu was asking for him! He responded without hesitation. His course of study must take second place to such a request. He caught the night train and at nine o'clock the next morning arrived in Kolhapur.

There followed several days of almost ceaseless activity. The sadhu was in great demand, not only by Christians, but by Hindus and Muslims as well. The day after his arrival in Kolhapur Vincent had to accompany him on a journey of sixty miles to a village where lived a little group of about a dozen Christians. The Sunday meeting held for this tiny minority attracted no attention until it was announced that the famous sadhu from North India, Sundar Singh, had arrived. A crowd gathered — three hundred of them, including Brahmins and Marathis, all wanting to see and hear him.

There was nothing for it but to hold the meeting in the open air. It was a new experience for Vincent, and he took his stand beside the sadhu with some trepidation. The sadhu spoke on the text 'Today is the day of salvation' and Vincent admitted afterwards that he had never heard such a sermon. But he interpreted clearly and without hesitation, although he was on his feet for over an hour. Then, as the sadhu sat down, with Vincent beside him, there was a stir in the crowd. Some of the Hindu men were talking together, then stood up and said,

'We know all about Christ. The missionaries have been telling us about him for twenty years. But now we understand truly that he is the only Saviour, and we want to accept him.' There were nine of them, and they indicated that they wanted to be baptised there and then, with their wives and children.

It was almost unbelievable, but it was true. There was no doubt about their sincerity, and their understanding of the step they were taking. The missionary who had escorted the sadhu and Vincent willingly performed the ceremony. At the evening meeting a wealthy Brahmin indicated that he, too, wanted to accept Christ.

It had been a memorable day, and when they were alone at last the sadhu told Vincent that he had never before seen people ready to become Christians through an interpreter. 'I urge you, if our beloved Lord calls you to do this work, never refuse,' he said earnestly, and then he produced a black velvet scarf on which were stitched in scarlet the words, 'Christ came to save sinners.' Handing it to Vincent with a smile he said,

'I've been wearing this for three years. I want you to accept it from me now, as a present.' It became Vincent's most treasured possession.

They spent several days in Kolhapur, and among the many invitations they received was one to go for three nights to listen to the boarders in a Girls' Hostel singing Christian lyrics, in the open air. It was quite cold, and as he sat there the sadhu wrapped himself round in the cotton shawl he always carried with him. The girls noticed this, and the following night presented him with a warm and expensive shawl. They had clubbed together to buy it for him, and he accepted it gratefully and graciously, wrapping it round himself immediately. He appeared in it the following night, too, for the final occasion. But as he and Vincent were on their way home, they saw an old man in tatters, trying to warm himself by a fire. The sadhu stopped, looked at him, then walked over, wrapped the shawl around the old man, and rejoined Vincent.

'He needs it more than I do,' was the only explanation he gave.

Vincent knew that the sadhu did not keep things for himself, and refused gifts of money. All he would accept was the train ticket to his next destination. On one occasion, when a gift of twenty-five rupees was handed to him as he boarded the train, he politely handed it back, saying he did not need it. His well-intentioned friends determined to give it to him, and threw the packet into his carriage as the train was starting.

The sadhu did not keep it for long. At one of the stops a beggar, shivering in his tattered clothes, came along the platform and stood with a skinny hand held out at the carriage door. 'The sadhu looked at the man for a short while, then lifted the packet of money and put it into his hands, to his great amazement,' Vincent reported later. He also mentioned that the sadhu strongly objected to collections being taken to defray his expenses at any of the meetings he attended. He was seeing at close range what he had already heard about the sadhu and his life of renunciation.

He was experiencing, too, a heartening sense of comradeship with him. Interpreting was a very exacting exercise, demanding unceasing concentration, and when, after a long train journey, they learned on arrival that a big meeting was planned to commence in an hour's time, Vincent confided to the sadhu that he was feeling quite frightened. He was so tired, he wondered how he would be able to interpret before what he knew would be a large and well-educated audience.

'Don't be afraid,' said the sadhu reassuringly. 'You are not going to interpret — the One you are serving will do that,' and then he suggested that they should pray. The two of them knelt together, and the sadhu prayed.

'Oh, that prayer went through and through my heart,' reported Vincent later. 'It was very short, but so charming, true, loving and full of faith, as if our Lord was with us.' Not only was the sermon interpreted satisfactorily that evening, but the following day Vincent stood three times beside the sadhu, each time interpreting sermons lasting over an hour. In addition, there was a steady stream of people coming to see the sadhu, asking questions that needed interpreting. Many well-educated Hindus were among those who came to hear him, and Vincent wrote,

'They seemed to have been taken up by the personality of the sadhu; his simple and true life, his way of speaking, his selflessness, all these produced a very great effect on the audience. As one of them remarked, "I never thought that among Indian Christians such a man could be found." '

Yet here again he encountered direct criticism from an outspoken missionary. One of the meetings arranged there in Ratnagiri was for the lawyers of the town, and when they arrived, bringing their families with them, there were about two hundred people present. After the meeting many of them moved forward, eager to speak to the sadhu, some even to do him homage. Two or three of the lawyers prostrated themselves before him and he immediately lifted them up, saying,

115

'Oh, don't do this!' But when others crowded round him, and women, wanting him to notice their children, reverently lifted his scarf and touched the children's heads with it, he merely smiled. The veneration with which the people treated him seemed excessive and out of place to one of the missionaries, and he said so.

'Why do you allow people to pay you this respect in all these ways?' he asked indignantly.

'I do not want this honour,' replied the sadhu. 'They do it out of their love for me.' The missionary was not satisfied.

'This honour belongs to Christ, not to you!'

Vincent David listened with some embarrassment to this verbal attack, wondering how the sadhu would counter it. He never forgot the sadhu's reply. There was no mock modesty about it. Quite mildly, but firmly, he said,

'Well, Sahib, I will tell you why I get this honour, and why I accept it. My beloved Jesus went to Jerusalem riding on an ass. The people took off their clothes and spread them on the road. It was the ass who walked on the clothes, not Jesus. The ass was honoured because he carried Jesus.

'I am like that ass. People honour me, not for my sake, but because I preach Christ . . .'

One night Vincent caught a glimpse of the source of the spiritual power that flowed through this man, not yet thirty years old, who was having such an influence on so many different types of people. He and the sadhu had been allocated a small, lonely cottage with a single room and a large verandah, and they had been warned to be on the lookout for snakes, as the place was infested with them. Vincent offered to sleep on the verandah, leaving the sadhu to occupy the room,

116

and during the night, hearing a gentle movement, he flashed on his torch to see a snake crawling along. It disappeared into the garden and Vincent decided that before going back to bed he would ensure that there were no snakes in the sadhu's room. Quietly he moved across the verandah, and shone his torch on the bed. To his surprise, it was empty. Then he shone it around the room, and there, in a corner, was the sadhu. He was sitting cross-legged, his hands clasped together, eyes closed, and his face aglow with joy. He was in prayer. Vincent flashed off his torch and returned silently to his bed, wondering.

The next morning he spoke about it. Why was the sadhu praying at that time, right in the middle of the night?

'When I'm on these preaching tours I do not find enough time during the day for prayer,' the sadhu replied. 'There are so many engagements.'

'Why do you need so much time for prayer?' Vincent persisted. He knew the sadhu well enough by now to ask intimate questions, and the opportunity to do so would soon be past. Within a few days their paths would diverge, as he went back to college in Poona, and the sadhu continued his tour to the far south. He had seen the sadhu in prayer in public, when leading a meeting, in smaller groups when interceding with others, and when the two of them had been together. He knew, too, of the sadhu's habit of rising early for private prayer. But there had been something different about that secret prayer in the silence of the night. Vincent was vaguely conscious of having glimpsed a depth of spiritual rapture beyond anything he had known. What was it?

The sadhu responded to the question quite readily. There was no mystery to be jealously guarded in what he did.

'It takes fifteen or twenty minutes for me to concentrate,' he admitted frankly. 'Then I begin to pray. But I do not use words.' He paused a moment, then continued more quietly, with instinctive reverence as he revealed an intimacy not all would be able to understand.

'I feel my beloved Jesus so close to me that I place my hands in his... When morning comes and I have to leave my prayer, it is an effort to break away from my beloved.'

The sadhu was expected to arrive in Madras on New Year's Day 1918, and he was booked to speak in the Memorial Hall that evening. The Christian community was agog to see and hear him. Very few in Madras had ever met him, but his name was well-known, so many stories had been told about him, not only of his adventures in Tibet, but also of his Christlike attitude towards those who had persecuted him, even attacked him physically. There was the man who had deliberately thrown sand into his eyes when he was preaching on the banks of the Ganges, another who had knocked him down and cut his face — and both had been brought to repentance as they saw his genuinely forgiving spirit, heard him praying for them. They had heard, too, of his influence over wild animals — there was the case of the black panther that stealthily watched the sadhu as he walked past, but did not attack him though the beast had killed several other people in the neighbourhood. The villagers all regarded the sadhu with awe after that, and listened willingly to his message, for undoubtedly he was a holy man, they said. And then there was the testimony of Shoran Singha, who spent a few days with the sadhu in a country area:

'One night, just before we went to bed, we noticed

lights moving in the valley, and the sadhu explained to me that men were probably in pursuit of a leopard...' Long after midnight, realising that the sadhu was no longer in the room, Shoran got up and looked out of the window. He knew that the sadhu often spent hours of the night in prayer under the starlit sky, but he remembered the leopard, and felt uneasy. 'A few yards from the house I saw the sadhu sitting, looking down into the deep valley. It was a beautiful night. The stars were shining brightly, a light wind rustled the leaves of the trees. For a few moments I watched the silent figure of the sadhu. Then my eyes were attracted by something moving on his right. An animal was coming towards him. As it got nearer I saw that it was a leopard. Choked with fear, I stood motionless near the window, unable even to call. Just then the sadhu turned his face towards the animal and held out his hand. As though it had been a dog, the leopard lay down and stretched out its head to be stroked...A short time afterwards the sadhu returned and was soon asleep, but I lay awake wondering what gave that man such power over wild animals.'

With stories like this to whet their appetite, it is not surprising that the sadhu was the main topic of conversation when Christian groups met in Madras. There was speculation about his appearance. Would he look like a Hindu ascetic, thin and austere, body and mind obviously under strict control? Perhaps he would exude an atmosphere of calm serenity like a Buddhist monk merging from a period of meditative contemplation? Or even the self-possessed dignity of a Roman Catholic or Anglican bishop? At any rate, they were sure that in himself he would not be like the European missionaries who had been imposing their own methods of church organisation on their congregations, and were producing a form of Christianity that was thoroughly un-Indian.

Some of the Christians in Madras were feeling very strongly about this. The gospel of Jesus Christ should be presented, not only in the spoken languages of India, but in the context of its culture and spiritual heritage as well. A group with this in mind had been formed called *Christo Samaj*. They wondered whether the sadhu would agree to have private conversations with individuals and groups. They hoped that he would, for there were things they wanted to know about what was going on in North India, as well as his experiences in Tibet.

The young lawyer, P. Chenchiah, was not among the small group that met the sadhu as he got off the train in a depressing drizzle of rain early in the morning, so the first sight he got of him was when he walked onto the platform in the crowded Memorial Hall. Like others, Chenchiah had wondered what he would look like but,

'The sadhu was unlike all the mental pictures I had formed of him — he was superior to all I had thought of him,' he reported many years later, when he was the Chief Judge in the State of Pudukatta. 'A tall young man, delivering his message with the fire of a prophet and the power of an apostle. The audience hung on his lips and never for a moment allowed their eyes to stray from that central figure.'

The sadhu's sermon, as always, was richly illustrated by incidents from his own experience and observation, vividly expressed in parable form. One which never failed to challenge his hearers was the occasion when he was battling his way along a pass on the Tibetan border, icy winds blowing, and the air

120

so cold he dared not stop to rest, weary though he was.

'I was not alone — a Tibetan was with me, and we were both finding the going hard. Then we came to a place where the path was very narrow, and we saw on a ledge some feet below a man lying crumpled and motionless. He had evidently slipped and fallen, and I said to my companion,

"We must go down and see if he is still alive. If so, we must help him to the village we're going to…"

"Help him?" my companion replied scornfully. "We've got ourselves to think of! We'd lose our own lives trying to save him." And he went on. I climbed to the ledge, found the man was alive, but unconscious, and managed to drag him up to the path. Then I had to get him on my back. It was difficult, but I did it, and staggered slowly along with my load.

'I could not go fast, but at least I was moving, and the exertion warmed me — and the warmth got through to the man on my back. Eventually I reached the village and got shelter for us both. We were both alive!

'…But on the way there I had passed another figure — it was my Tibetan companion, lying by the path. He was stone cold, and dead.'

Then the sadhu brought home his point.

'Whoever wants to save his life will lose it, but whoever loses his life will find it.'

He stayed in Madras for a fortnight, preaching daily in a number of churches and halls. Sometimes the crowds that gathered were so great that people had to be turned away. In addition to the meetings there were private interviews with individuals and groups, and one of these Chenchiah reported very fully in a local newspaper called *The Christian Patriot*.

'It was a characteristically Indian scene,' he wrote.

121

'The sadhu was in the centre and all sat around him, some on chairs, some on the ground.' They talked quite freely, asking him questions, and were particularly eager to know more about the Secret Sanyasi Mission, and he told them,

'I first came to know of the existence of this secret mission through the Maharishi at Kailash, and although I do not belong to the order myself, I can bear testimony to the great Christian work that is being done by them. In my wanderings in North India I have been greatly struck with the sacrifice and love with which the message of our Lord is being spread.

'Their method of work is purely Indian, and to a large extent individual. Secrecy is enjoined on the disciple, with the result that sometimes not even the members of a family are aware of a change of faith, except as it manifests itself in character and behaviour. The secrecy under which the whole work is carried on is in no way detrimental to their faith. I have known many families which put Christians to shame, by their Christian life and zeal.'

He went on to tell them of a time when he was preaching on the banks of the Ganges, and heard about a Hindu preacher who lived near by, and was attracting great crowds. 'You should go and visit him,' people said, and one day he was able to meet him when he was alone.

'I am a disciple of Christ,' he told the Hindu preacher, and to his amazement the man promptly embraced him and said,

'Brother, we are doing the same work.'

'But I've never heard you preach Christ!'

The answer he received was illuminating.

'Is any farmer so foolish as to sow without first preparing the ground?' he asked. 'I first try to awaken in my hearers a sense of spiritual values. Then, when a hunger and thirst for righteousness is created, I present Christ.' The Hindu preacher went on to tell him that he had baptised about twelve educated Hindus during the past year, and opening his satchel showed him the Bible he always carried with him.

'The great need today is that the Church should have a broad vision,' the sadhu said. 'The Christian should transcend the limitations of sect and creed and be prepared to recognise the Spirit of the Lord in whatever form it may manifest itself. The Secret Sanyasi Mission has the blessing of our Lord, and though it has taken a form we are not accustomed to, yet its leaders are doing great things in this country...beyond the pale of our conventional churches.'

The sadhu withdrew after that, and the group dispersed, rather quietly. The young Indian in his saffron robe and with his bare feet might preach with the fire of a prophet and the power of an apostle — but as he moved quietly and naturally among ordinary people and talked with them, there was that about him that reminded them of the meekness and gentleness of Christ.

Young R. R. Rajamani was still a schoolboy when he had an interview lasting twenty minutes with the sadhu. It had been arranged by his headmaster, and it involved a twelve-mile journey by bullock cart to get to it. The headmaster went in first to see the sadhu, and when the time came for Rajamani to go in he was suddenly overcome to find himself with so famous a man, about whom he had heard some strange tales. The sadhu smiled at him, and said kindly,

'Do you want to ask me anything?'

All thoughts fled. The only thing that came to mind was what he had heard the other boys saying about the sadhu's eating habits.

'Please, sir, is it true that you only eat chilli powder?' he blurted out.

The sadhu was taken aback for a moment, then threw back his head and roared with laughter.

'No, boy!' he exclaimed, and went on chuckling as he said,

'No, I eat food just like you do. Is there anything else?'

Still Rajamani could think of nothing but the stories he had heard in the playground.

'Is it true that you keep clean without washing? That you never have to bathe, and never have to get your clothes washed?'

The sadhu laughed again. He seemed to be enjoying this interview with its revelations of the sort of legends that were being invented about him.

'No, I perspire a lot,' he admitted reassuringly. 'I need to bathe often, and wash my clothes too.' Rajamani relaxed. The sadhu was evidently quite human, after all, and the conversation continued along a more serious line. He wanted to know about the Maharishi in Kailash, and when he heard more about that famous Christian hermit, and the journey necessary to take to reach him, he said earnestly,

'Oh, sir, let me come with you!'

'You're not strong enough for such long journeys yet,' was the reply. 'This sort of life is no bed of roses.' It was not to be embarked on unless God ordained it. 'But one day the Lord will call you, and you will be able to go forth in his service, as I have done.' Then they knelt together, and the sadhu prayed for him.

Many years later, when Rajamani returned to that very place to preach with Bakht Singh, as one of his senior colleagues, he remembered that prayer.

Mr Daniel, the founder of the Layman's Evangelical Fellowship, was another who as a young man was inspired by the sadhu. He not only went to hear the sadhu himself, but cycled round with handbills announcing the meetings to be held, urging every one of his classmates to go. Daniel longed to speak to him personally, and the interpreter arranged a meeting between them. The outcome was that the sadhu, recognising the boy's unusually deep spirituality, took an interest in him, and invited him to accompany him on the next stage of his tour. Daniel, in his enthusiasm, wanted to go further. Like Rajamani he wanted to go to Tibet, intimating that he was prepared to die as a martyr there. The sadhu's reply was brief but unconsciously revealing. He spoke as one who had known physical hardship and suffering, loneliness and rejection, secret and open hostility, long days and nights of strain and weariness, mental exhaustion and spiritual conflict over many years, all for the sake of the Name.

'To die as a martyr for Christ is easy. To live for Christ is hard.'

HEAVEN

In heaven no one can ever be a hypocrite, for all can see the lives of others as they are...The degree of goodness reached by the soul of a righteous man is known by the brightness that radiates from his whole appearance, for character and nature show themselves in the form of various glowing rainbow-like colours of great glory.

In heaven there is no jealousy. All are glad to see the spiritual elevation and glory of others, and without any motives of self-interest try at all times truly to serve one another.

The Spiritual World

Chapter

10

As the train drew to a standstill at Trivandram station Sundar stood at the open door of his carriage, his eyes passing quickly over the group of Indians eagerly awaiting him, to light with a smile on the only westerner present — the missionary with whom he was to stay during his brief visit to this southernmost part of India. They had not yet personally met, but the warmth of the invitation he had received from Arthur Parker and his wife had encouraged him, and when the crowd of Indian Christians who had gathered to meet him were persuaded to leave him free to wash and have a meal, immediately he felt at home with them.

Arthur and Rebecca Parker had been in India for thirty years, and they loved its people. What they had heard about the young sadhu had given them a great desire to meet him, and within a few minutes of welcoming him into their home Rebecca in particular had taken him to her heart. Although he stayed in Trivandram only two or three days on that occasion, and the time was taken up with meetings and interviews with individuals and groups, she managed to do for him the sort of things a mother would do for a son, ensuring that he had time to eat his food in quiet and that he was supplied with all the things he might need in his room. She herself was always available, ready and receptive for anything he might divulge about himself.

A few days after he left she wrote him a little note, with a gift 'in happy memory' of his stay, and so a correspondence started which lasted for the rest of his life. The third letter he wrote commenced, 'My dear mother,' and from that time on she was always 'mother' to him. It was a unique relationship in his life, filling the natural as well as spiritual gap left by his own mother. For all his conscious need of seclusion to spend time alone with God, for all his delight in the glories and variety of creation, there was a human side of his nature that reached out for human companionship. He was a man who had many friends, some whom he lovingly called 'brother', but Rebecca Parker was the only woman he called 'mother'.

From Trivandram he travelled north to take part in the Mar Thoma Syrian Convention, held annually during the dry season on a large island at the bend of the river that flows through north Travancore. As usual, a booth large enough to hold over 20,000 people had been erected, and before dawn every day a man with a stentorian voice broke the silence as he passed round the encampment crying,

'Praise be to God. Praise to the Son of God!'

It was the signal to rise and pray. From all over the encampment came the sound of hundreds of voices chanting prayers in ancient Syrian tunes, rising to a roaring crescendo, then slowly dying down into silence again.

Then came the meetings, with thousands of men,

women and children swarming into the great booth to sit on the sandy ground, the women, all in white, sitting on one side, men and boys in front and on the other side. In the centre was the platform with two seats occupied by the two bishops, resplendent in their robes of red or purple satin, with gold belts and elaborate headdresses. In front of them, sitting cross-legged on the platform, were the clergy of the church, and in front of them, also cross-legged, Sundar took his place.

It was a deeply moving experience for him. He had heard about the great numbers of Christians in South India, had seen them meeting in their hundreds in Trivandram, after that in their thousands at the Jacobite Syrian Convention, but this surpassed them both for sheer numbers — numbers that increased as the days of the convention week passed. He realised that this sort of gathering had been going on for years, decades, even centuries, for the historic Syrian Church of Malabar, divided now into the Roman, the Jacobite and the Mar Thoma claimed to have been founded by the Apostle Thomas. The gathering of so many people claiming to be Christian was encouraging in a way, until he remembered the countless villages to which he had gone in northern and central India, where the gospel of Jesus Christ had never been heard. As the Bishop pronounced, one by one, topics for prayer, the quiet murmurs from the devout company were solemnising — but how was it that so very, very few of the young men among them were responding to the commission given nearly two thousand years before to 'Go — tell the gospel to every creature?'

When the time came for him to preach he rose to his feet and gazed silently for a moment at the vast concourse before him. The silence with which all eyes were fixed on him was intense, for here, too, his reputation had gone before him, and there was that about his presence that awed them. Then as he began to preach he could not forbear to remind them that centuries ago God had entrusted to them his word, had committed to them the gospel of his Son. But they had failed even to pass the Good News on to their own fellow countrymen. And what had been the result? God had been forced to call men, and women too, from far countries like America and England to do the work they should have done. Yet India had had the gospel hundreds of years before these other countries.

'Oh, young men, wake up! See how many souls are perishing around you! Is it not your duty to save them?

'Glory to God! He has given you a priceless opportunity to be saved, and to save others. Be good soldiers of Jesus Christ. Go forward in full armour. Crush Satan's work and victory will be yours!'

Then he sounded a note of very solemn warning.

'If you are careless now, you will never get another chance. Whatever you have to do, do it now! Do it now! For you will never pass through the field of battle again.

'The day is fast approaching when you will see the martyrs in their glory, martyrs who gave health, wealth, even life itself to win souls for Christ. They have done much. What have you done? Oh, may we not blush with shame in that day!'

His challenge came at a good time, for the Syrian church in Travancore had already become aware of its failure to evangelise, and was sending out a small trickle of missionaries to other parts of India. But he had something further to say. It was about what he saw as the greatest weakening influence in the church in South India. He said,

'We can compare India to a man. The Himalayas are his head, South India is his feet, Punjab his right hand and Bengal his left. If this man is to stand firm he has to stand on South India, his feet. South India is indeed fit for this. The Christians of South India are very advanced, in numbers as well as in education. But though many of their churches are self-supporting, and though this man can stand on his feet, he is unable to walk now. What is the reason? I saw a Jew in the state of Cochin. He stood, but could not walk. Why? Because he had elephantiasis which made his legs swollen and heavy.

'Elephantiasis! The Indian Church is unable to proclaim the gospel all over India and to save the whole country because of the elephantiasis of the Indian Church in the south. Caste distinction is like elephantiasis. Class distinction is its main weakness. Through this and other causes there is a lack of love, and therefore lack of anxiety to save others. If this disease is healed the Church of South India will be used as an instrument...'

If he spoke sternly about the weaknesses he saw, Sundar spoke earnestly and tenderly enough as he alluded to the recent reform movement in the ancient church, urging his hearers to rise to the call, and send the light to the millions who were still dying in darkness. And as Rebecca Parker, who was present at the Convention, reported,

'The sadhu drew greater crowds than usual, so that before the end of the week the booth had to be enlarged, and at the final meeting no fewer than 32,000 people gathered to hear his last message.'

The Parkers were not the only lasting ties of friendship that he forged in that visit to South India. Dewan Bahadur A. S. Appasamy was a lawyer, and a former Hindu. He was delighted to meet the young sadhu who was having so wide and effective a ministry, and realising that Sundar needed a rest after his ceaseless round of meetings, invited him to stay in his home in the hills. Here he could have all the opportunity he could wish for to be quiet, to wander through the thickly wooded grounds with their acacia and eucalyptus trees, where a little stream flowed quietly, and where he could enjoy bird-watching to his heart's content.

Sundar accepted the invitation gratefully. He had found the heat and humidity of the south very trying. As he wrote to a friend in the north, he felt like a dissolving lump of salt — 'though I am willing to melt like salt if only the south is salted!' It was a relief to be in the cool of the hills. Furthermore, it gave him the opportunity to study English. His experiences in the south had impressed on him the advantage it would be to speak this language, which was widely used and understood. It would relieve him of the necessity of relying on interpreters at all his meetings. Not all had proved as satisfactory as Vincent David. Some of them had proved to be, as he quaintly put it, 'interrupters more than interpreters!'

Those were enjoyable days for Sundar. The Appasamy family did everything possible to make him comfortable, urging him unsuccessfully to suggest any changes he would like in the diet. He had no preferences, he assured them; he liked everything they provided. Only after a good deal of pressing did they elicit from him that though he liked milk better than tea, and tea than coffee, what he really wanted was for the liquid to be as hot as possible. The temperature mattered more than the taste. It became a common sight to see him holding the silver tumbler in which his drink was served, wrapped in the end of his turban because it was too hot for his hand, but smilingly drinking it down with a gulp.

He often bathed in the stream, washing his clothes first and putting them on bushes to dry. After his bathe he rubbed oil on himself 'which made his fair body glisten as if it were moulded out of twenty-carat gold', as Appasamy's son, who shared a cottage with him, described it. He also noticed the care with which Sundar tied his turban. It was about ten yards long, and Sundar always wound it round his head in a certain way, unconsciously betraying the high social class from which his Sikh ancestors came. The habits of tidiness learned in the Singh courtyard in Rampur were never forgotten.

Sundar spent six weeks in the Appasamys' hospitable home, and in addition to studying English had many talks with his host. Mr Appasamy had retired early from his profession as a lawyer in order to devote himself to Christian activities and prayer. An earnest man, deeply concerned for the evangelisation of his own country, he saw in Sundar's manner of life and manner of preaching, the way in which it could be achieved. With its strong appeal to the soul of the Indian it was proving far more effective than any amount of church and mission organisation.

But one man alone could not evangelise the whole of India. More of his type were needed, and he put before Sundar the idea that was formulating in his mind. If Sundar would agree to his proposal, a centre could be established for the training of Christian sadhus to do the same sort of work as Sundar was doing. In this way he would be multiplying himself, and millions more would hear the message he was so eager to proclaim.

Others were to make the same suggestions to him from time to time, but although Sundar could not fail to see the reasonableness of the idea, he was never convinced that it was God's calling for him. He pursued his way of renunciation alone, as a simple sadhu whose aim was to preach Christ.

He set off next to cross to the beautiful island of Ceylon (now Sri Lanka) where a public meeting in the American Mission compound in Jaffna had been arranged. All the Christian schools and colleges in the vicinity were closed to free the students to attend, and with non-Christians as well as Christians in the booth of plaited coconut leaves that had been erected, there were 2,000 people gathered to see and hear him. This meeting was followed by others in the Jaffna peninsula, and everywhere he went crowds gathered, some people following him from place to place. The arrangements for this tour had been undertaken by a young theological student who had just graduated from the United Theological College in Bangalore, and thirty years later he recalled:

'My close association with the sadhu just as I was commencing my ministry was providential, as I found later, because it made such a deep impression on me, and coloured the outlook and aim of my life and work as a preacher of the gospel. His frequent references to prayer in his addresses and the remarkable way the good news of Jesus Christ our Lord was reflected in all its purity and simplicity in the soul of an Indian like me, and almost of my age, were a great challenge to me, pointing to me the need for unreserved surrender to Christ and entire dependence upon him — lessons I am ever grateful to have learned from the sadhu as I commenced my ministry.'

From Jaffna Sundar went to Colombo. A wealthy businessman there had arranged for a series of meetings to be held in a large hall, and here again, crowds gathered.

During this period in Sundar's life he was involved in two cases of miraculous healing. One was of a woman who was so mentally deranged (or demon possessed) that at times she had to be chained to prevent her from doing something violent. She had heard about the sadhu, and one day, realising from the noise in the street that he was passing by, she shouted,

'My helper has come to relieve me!' She was healed immediately, although Sundar knew nothing about it until the woman's husband told him. When he was told he offered a special prayer of thanksgiving in the church where he was preaching.

The other case, which occurred in Colombo, was different. The mother of a boy who had had a serious operation, and whose life hung in the balance, came to ask him to go and visit her son in hospital. Sundar did not go immediately, but the following day asked to be taken there, and when he saw the boy he enquired, through an interpreter,

'What is it that you want me to do?'

'I want you to put your hand on my head and pray for me,' was the answer.

'I am not God,' said Sundar gently. 'I cannot heal you, but Jesus can. You must pray to him.'

'I know,' the boy responded immediately. 'All the same, please do as I ask...'

Sundar yielded, but explained that he would prefer to pray in his own language, Hindustani, rather than in English, and as the boy nodded he put his hands on his head, closed his eyes, and prayed.

The result was startling. Within a short time the boy's temperature went up so high that the nurses were alarmed. His parents were sent for 'in case anything should happen.'

What happened was that after an hour the temperature came down to normal, and a couple of days later the boy was pronounced completely healed.

News of this spread like wildfire. More attention than ever was focussed on Sundar — not because of his preaching, but because he was now appearing as a wonder-worker, one who could perform miracles.

It worried him. Again and again he asserted that it was not he who had healed the boy. 'I tried to get them to see it was the power of Christ in answer to prayer that had healed the boy.' Nothing he said seemed to change their attitude, and eventually he came to a decision which some of his friends believed was a mistake.

'As they would not be convinced, I determined not to do it again. I felt that it would encourage superstition and distract from the gospel I had to preach.' From that time he refrained from exercising the gift of healing he undoubtedly possessed, fearing that it would divert attention to himself and physical healing, and away from spiritual healing through faith in Christ alone.

One of his closest friends, reviewing his life and service years later, observed that it was a great pity that he had made this decision. and that his influence would have been even greater if, like his Master whom he loved so devotedly, he had shown the same compassion towards those who suffered physically.

Had Sundar followed the advice of his friends he would have started a training centre for Christian sadhus, and by demonstrating his healing gift would have attracted even more people than were already coming to his meetings. What the final outcome would have been is open to conjecture. As far as Sundar himself was concerned, once he was convinced of the path to which he believed God was pointing, he did not change his mind, and simply went forward along the same lines as before. His calling was to preach rather than to teach, and the effect of his personality and manner of life was not so much to instruct as to inspire.

After his visit to Ceylon he went back to Trivandram to stay for a few days with the Parkers. Rebecca Parker, whose main concern was for the women of Travancore, had conceived the idea of writing a book for them, based on the experiences and teaching of Sadhu Sundar Singh. This, she believed, would be a source of help and inspiration to them — a book printed in their own language of Malayalam, about one of their own countrymen whom they had actually seen and heard, and who had already made so deep an impression on them. He had agreed to supply her with the necessary material, and during the week he was with her Rebecca Parker was busy with her pen, scribbling down his answers to her questions, rapidly noting his reminiscences and observations. They had no idea, as they sat together over what was to them a simple, congenial, and comparatively unimportant task, to what it would lead, and how widely the message of his life would be spread.

They thought it would only be of local interest, but when friends of the Parkers heard about the book they suggested that instead of being confined to the Malayalam language it should be produced in English. This was done, and *Sadhu Sundar Singh: Called of God* was printed in 1918. There was an immediate demand for it, and the following year it was reprinted twice. After that there was a steady flow of reprints, with additional material, and eventually it was translated into a large number of other languages as well. Fifty years after it was first published, it was still in print, proving to be one of the means by which the Sikh schoolboy from a remote village in the Punjab became a world figure.

SONS OF LIGHT

When the souls of men arrive in the world of spirits the good at once separate from the evil. In the world all are mixed together, but it is not so in the spiritual world. I have many times seen that when the spirits of the good — the sons of light — enter into the world of spirits they first of all bathe in the impalpable air, like waters of a crystal clear ocean, and in this way they find an intense and exhilarating refreshment... Wonderfully cleansed and refreshed and fully purified, they enter into the world of glory and light, where they will ever remain in the presence of their dear Lord, and in the fellowship of innumerable saints and angels.

SONS OF DARKNESS

How different from these are the souls of those whose lives have been evil! Ill at ease in the company of the sons of light, and tormented by the all-revealing light of glory, they struggle to hide themselves in places where their impure and sin-stained natures will not be seen. From the lowest and darkest part of the world of spirits a black and evil-smelling smoke arises, and in their effort to hide themselves from the light, these sons of darkness rush down, and cast themselves headlong into it...

The Spiritual World

11

'Do you recognise me?'

As Sundar looked at the questioner a light came into his eyes, and there flashed into his memory the time when he had been poisoned, and the dispenser from the local hospital had been called to see him.

'Yes, of course I remember you,' he said, and added whimsically, 'You came to see me on my death bed!' Then he learned how that experience of his miraculous healing had resulted in the dispenser starting to read the Bible, leading to him putting his faith in Christ. 'So now I am serving the Lord as a missionary here in Burma,' he explained.

Sundar himself was in Burma on a preaching tour. It was his first time away from the Indian sub-continent, the beginning of what was to be the most remarkable period in his life, when he travelled alone to countries in the Far East, to Europe, America and Australia, clad as always in his saffron robe and wearing sandals on his bare feet. With no influential patron, no well-financed organisation behind him, refusing the expensive gifts and large sums of money that were offered to him, he was to be a contemporary evidence of the reality of living by faith in God. Everywhere he went doors opened for him to preach, and by the end of 1922, when he returned to India never to go overseas again, invitations were reaching him at such a rate it was difficult even to reply to them all, let alone accede to the requests made. He had become an international figure.

By 1918, in his own country he had already become well-known and respected. After his return from South India and Ceylon he had spent several days recovering from a bad bout of influenza in the house of the famous poet, Dr Rabindranath Tagore. In other countries all that was known about him was what had appeared in books and magazines, or through reports brought back by missionaries and others. His visit to Burma was preceded by that of his friend, Bishop Lefroy, and this helped to pave the way for him there.

'Praise the Lord that he has blessed the meetings beyond our expectations in the different parts of Burma,' he wrote to a friend as he was on the eve of leaving, adding the appreciative words, 'You have a great share in this work for our Lord. I am very thankful to you for your kind help and your prayers.'

That his stay in the country influenced others besides the usual run of people attending Christian meetings was evidenced by the provision of a free passage from Rangoon to Singapore by the owner of the steamship company.

In Singapore Sundar encountered one of the minor crises of his life. In that cosmopolitan city he had expected that a Hindustani speaker would easily be found to interpret for him, but he was dismayed to discover when he arrived at the first meeting that there was no one who could do it. There was nothing for it but to preach in the language most commonly understood — English. He had been applying his mind to the study of English for months, but had been very hesitant even to use it in conversation. The prospect of standing on a platform and preaching in it filled him with dismay, and as he admitted afterwards, he felt as though there was a sort of earthquake in him. 'As when fire and other matters under the earth cannot escape there is an earthquake, so when thoughts in my heart have no means of escape, my heart quakes!' But he went through with it, and later referred to Singapore as having provided him with the practice he needed to preach in the most universal of languages.

From Singapore he went to the cities of Ipoh, Kuala Lumpur and Penang. In Penang, where he preached in the Empire Theatre, his address was briefly translated into the languages of the three main ethnic groups — Malay, Chinese and Indian. A special meeting for Sikhs was convened in St George's Chapel, where he was able to preach, to his relief, in Hindustani, at the close of which he was invited to go and speak in the Sikh temple.

'Without money, without home, clad in the simple saffron-coloured robe, he started tramping from place to place, like a friar of the Middle Ages, preaching the gospel of Jesus Christ and commending it by the self-sacrifice of his life.' So ran a report which gave a brief description of his life in India, and went on to describe his visit to Malaya. 'According to Christ's injunction, "Into whatsoever house ye enter, there remain, eating and drinking such things as they give," he accepts any hospitality offered him, whether simple or rich food, rickshaw or motor-car, third or first class carriage. These things to him are matters of indifference: but there appears to be a danger lest such accessories as these, if multiplied, should tend to obscure the meaning and purpose and reality of his life as a sadhu. His message undoubtedly makes a strong appeal to Indians, who flock to hear him. His language is simple and clear, his illustrations homely, yet often profound, and usually extremely apposite and illuminating.'

Sundar was a good correspondent. In spite of all the adjustments necessary as he moved from place to place, and the strain of speaking at meeting after meeting, often through interpreters, he managed to keep in touch with his friends and continue his contributions to magazines and papers. At the beginning of February 1919 he wrote to *The Christian Patriot* from Singapore announcing that he was about to set out for Japan and China. He had received invitations from Christians in both countries to come and speak at some meetings that could be specially arranged, and had decided to accept them. In Singapore he was well on the way to the Far East, and he hoped to be able to get to his mission field of Tibet by way of China. He would be going there in April or May, he said. (He little knew the difficulties of travel that would be involved — China had not the network of railways he was accustomed to in India.)

He was evidently looking even further afield after that, for he continued,

'God has opened a great field of work for me. I have already received many calls from America and Europe.' Then he added what was, in his case, a very sincere request:

'So I shall be very grateful if brethren will continue to help me through their prayers.'

So to Japan and China he went, countries in which his colourful apparel was oddly at variance with the more sober dress of their inhabitants. In China especially, where all clothes were confined to various shades of dull blue, and where everyone wore cloth-soled shoes, the appearance of a tall, bearded man in a tangerine-coloured turban and a saffron robe, whose feet were bare but for sandals, was almost like a visitant from another planet. Even westerners in their suits and ties and leather shoes paled into insignificance beside him. Fortunately his appearances in public places were comparatively few, though as soon as he was seen he was immediately surrounded by the inevitable crowd of silently staring spectators.

Arrangements were made by the China Inland Mission for him to speak in churches in several places, and the son of Hudson Taylor, its founder, interpreted for him in some of them. He visited Peking, where he preached in the cathedral which was packed to capacity, and spoke also in Nanking, Hankow and Shanghai.

In Japan he spoke in Tokyo, Kobe, Osaka and Kyoto. Comparatively little had been done in the way of preliminary arrangements, so the meetings were small, but as always, the impression he made was very deep. In Kobe some of the young people, after seeing and hearing him, engaged for the first time in evangelistic work. It was perhaps typical of the enthusiasm of youth that they also decided that, like the sadhu, they would not wear socks!

As in other places, his appearance reminded people of the pictures they had seen of Christ. One girl, suddenly seeing him walk across the campus of her school rushed to the Principal's room and bursting in said breathlessly,

'Teacher! Teacher! Here comes Jesus! Here comes Jesus!'

Although the meetings he addressed in China and

Japan were small compared with those in other countries, there was a reason for this. Elsewhere his audiences had been largely composed of Indians, among whom he was already quite famous. In the Far East his name at the time was virtually unknown. Not until later, when books about him were widely published and circulated, was it realised that an Indian Christian outstanding in world history had been among them.

As far as Sundar himself was concerned, he expressed himself amazed that God should have taken him to other countries and other races to preach Christ. As he wrote to a friend,

'I never realised before that God will make me, an unworthy servant, to be his witness before the different nations of the world. His Name be praised! Amen!'

He was a perceptive observer of the people he had gone to, and summed them up succinctly,

'The Burmese are of the Mongolian type and are Buddhists, and for this reason they have no true idea of God. It is difficult to make them understand, for in their language they seem to have no word that rightly expresses our idea of God. But they are a simple people, and their temples are all open to visitors. They are not bigoted as are Hindus and Muslims. But the Hindus here not only attend meetings themselves, but they bring their wives with them!

'Japan has plunged herself in the soul-killing floods of western materialism. Her eyes are filled with visions of worldly greatness. She is in the fury of making money and has no ear for the word of God. All religious appeals fall flat on the Japanese...not even a nominal condemnation of things which would have shocked the moral susceptibilities of an ordinary Indian. The worst of it is, Japan does not even take

Buddhism seriously. Her temples are thronged with tourists and guides more than devotees.

'In China things are not so bad. The Chinaman has still reverence and love for religion. He is capable of the highest spiritual development.

'In China and Japan one great obstacle to the acceptance of Christianity that is present in India, the caste difficulty, is non-existent. That makes it easier socially for a man to accept Christ. Some of the highest officers in China are Christians, and good Christians, too. With regard to students, there is a danger of testing the growth of Christianity among them by the number of pledge cards they sign. I don't much believe in it. When I addressed a meeting in China, nearly all the students signed cards promising to study the claims of Christ. I know enough of human nature to believe that not more than one-hundredth of them will be able to keep their promise. But, taking all things into account, the Chinese are more open to persuasion than the Japanese.'

Sundar's hope of getting to Tibet through China had to be abandoned. He learned that the Chinese were fighting with the Tibetans on the border, and it would be useless for him to attempt to get into the country that way, so he gave up the idea. He obtained a berth on a steamer from Shanghai, and arrived back in Madras on 9 May 1919, where a meeting was hurriedly arranged for him in the Memorial Hall. He spoke on the text 'You will receive power when the Holy Ghost comes on you; and you will be my witnesses...to the ends of the earth.' His subject was the solemn obligation for every Christian to bear witness for Christ — and the privilege it is for human beings to bear the cross for him — a privilege denied to the angels in heaven. He concluded his address with the words:

'I am going to the hills and to Tibet! It is quite uncertain whether I shall be able to return, so serious are some of the risks attending the journey and my work in the regions beyond. Even if I do not see you again in this world, I hope to meet you in heaven amidst the revelation of a new life and its surroundings. I wish you good-bye till we meet again.'

Little wonder if many eyes were moist as he turned and made his way from the platform.

In the event, his journey into the Tibetan region was delayed, for two reasons. From Madras he went to Simla and set out from there for the Tibetan border, but on the way he injured his foot, and when he arrived at Kotgarh, some fifty miles from Simla, he had to stop and rest it. There was another reason for his delay there. During his absence in the Far East two groups of people had decided to take up his offer to escort those who were prepared to do so, to go and see the Maharishi in Kailash. One was a group of Indians and Singhalese, the other three women missionaries. Not until he reached Kotgarh did he know anything about the arrangements they had made to meet him somewhere else. In both cases their rather impractical plans had to be dropped, although the three intrepid women got as far as a village in the snow mountains called Badrinath, distinguished by a golden-roofed temple 'swarming with holy men and women'. After waiting there a week for Sundar, who knew nothing about it, they decided to abandon the plan and returned home.

As for Sundar, an attack of fever delayed him still further, and not until the beginning of July was he able to continue his journey into the mountains. He was accompanied by a young Tibetan Christian connected with the Moravian Mission, and together they spent about two months in the vast, barren region, dotted here and there with villages similar to Badrinath, but scattered so widely there were days on end when they saw no one but a shepherd or two in the distance, tending flocks of sheep. 'We slept out on the open plain when the cold was so intense that all feeling went out of the body and we became numb all over.'

On this journey they encountered little or no active opposition from the lamas who in some places received them very well, listening attentively to Sundar as well as discussing with him their own religious beliefs. And on one occasion, noticing that his hair had grown too long for comfort, they obligingly cut it for him, using a pair of sheep shears instead of scissors.

Nevertheless, the lives of some of the lamas stirred him with horror, when he saw that their claim to celibacy was a mere cover-up for promiscuity, while the blatant practice of homosexuality among others filled him with disgust.

'All sorts of evil customs and horrible wickedness prevail, the very mention of which is impossible here,' he wrote in a long letter to Rebecca Parker after his return. But on the other hand he was moved by what he saw of the hermits, and the lengths to which they went hoping to obtain the peace of ultimate oblivion. 'They shut themselves in a dark room, some for months, some for years, some for the whole of life. They are so shut away that they never see the sun and never come out of doors, but always sitting in the dark they continue turning a prayer wheel in their hand just as if they were living in a grave.

'In these small rooms there is a tiny window or hole through which the people pass food to these hermits. I tried to get into conversation with them, but never

149

had a proper opportunity.' The best he could do was to put some Scripture portions through the tiny windows in the hope that the occupants of the cells would read them, if ever they emerged alive from the blackness in which they existed. Sundar was seeing something of the moral and spiritual darkness that prevails under Satan's rule in the country which, as the Abbés Huc and Gabet described it, 'the enemy of all good seems to have chosen for the seat of his empire.'

Sundar's letter, written at Rebecca Parker's request for a full and detailed account of his journey, contained some vivid descriptions of the places he and his companion passed through. At one time they were above the tree line, where the air was so icy cold it was painful to breathe, and 'the beating of our hearts sounded in our ears. Here is a great glacier in which many people have lost their lives.' There were streams and rivers to be crossed, always bitterly cold, while the human habitations they eventually reached were very small, dirty, and unbearably smelly. In most places the only food obtainable was parched barley flour and buttered tea. One region they visited was bandit-ridden, and although they had good opportunities for preaching they were warned it was not safe to proceed any further without gun or sword.

'I replied that I had only a blanket and the sword of God, which is the Bible, but that the Lord of Life was with me…therefore thanks to him we went through that dreadful place preaching among murderers…yet not a single thing happened to give us trouble of any kind.'

His letter, which ran to many pages, not only contained information about the people's life and religious beliefs, but a brief historical outline of what he had learned of the history of Tibetan Buddhism in the country.

'Concerning the true God these people know nothing, but in their religion they have a kind of Trinity which is called Sangi Kunchek, or Buddha God; Lama Kunchek or Priest God; and Ghho Kunchek or Scripture God. Buddhism entered Tibet about AD 629 in the time of King Shang Taing Suganpo, and Lamaism was founded in AD 749 by Padmasambhave, who started the first monastery near Lhasa.

'In the year AD 1640 a Mongolian prince, Gusari Khan conquered Tibet and made a present to the Grand Lama of Drepung Monastery with the title of Dalai or Ocean who thus became the first King-Priest and is known as the Dalai Lama. His name was Magwan Lobang. Being very ambitious and wanting to combine the rule of State with the Church he declared himself an incarnation of the famous Chenrezing Avalokitesvara, the tutelary deity of Tibet. The Tibetans were no doubt delighted to have as ruler an incarnation of such a divinity and the scheme worked well, but in order not to offend the older, and in one sense superior, Lama of Troshi Shumpho, he declared this lama an incarnation of Amitabha...a higher deity, yet it is an impassive deity who cannot meddle with worldly affairs which are left to his spiritual son, represented by the Dalai Lama of Tibet.'

Rebecca Parker's first little book was in such demand that another edition was called for, and in it she incorporated the whole of this letter. The name of Sadhu Sundar Singh, and his journeys into the mysterious country of Tibet, with all the hardships that such journeys involved, were becoming more and more widely known, and brought a challenge to the readers as they came on the words,

'In all these difficulties there was this great comfort, that this was the cross of Christ, and was necessary for the salvation of souls. For me Christ forsook heaven, and took upon himself the burden of the cross, so that if I have left India to come into Tibet on his behalf to claim souls for him, it is not a great thing to do. But if I had not come it would have been a dreadful thing, for this is a divine command.'

He drew a lesson from what he had seen of the hermits, voluntarily incarcerated in those dark cells, too, for 'if these people will endure such suffering in order to attain Nirvana in which there is no future life or heavenly happiness nor any hope, believing that salvation lies in exterminating desires and spirit and life, how much more shall we not take up the cross with joy for Christ — the joy of our entrance into eternal life and of his great service who has given and will give us all things?'

Meanwhile Sundar himself, returning to preach in the towns and villages of the Punjab, arrived at his father's home in Rampur. His father's attitude towards him had changed considerably in recent months, and he was sure enough of a welcome when he entered the familiar Singh courtyard. But on this occasion the change was complete. His father greeted him with the news that he wanted to become a Christian.

It was one of the greatest joys of Sundar's life to see this answer to his incessant prayer to God for his father. Although Sher Singh never came out as clearly as his son, Sundar could now speak to him freely about his own spiritual experiences and receive a ready response. There was something on his mind which he was glad to talk over with one who was so close to him by natural as well as spiritual ties. He believed God was calling him to go to England.

His own desire had been to go to the Holy Land and

actually see the places where his Master had walked, but while he was thinking and praying about this the 'call' had come. It was to England, not Palestine, that he should go.

'Then I will pay for your passage,' said his father. That was enough for Sundar. He applied immediately to a shipping firm, booked a second-class cabin on a liner due to leave Bombay on 16 January 1920 and berth in Liverpool on 10 February, and set off alone for the English-speaking world. While the other passengers were superintending the disposal of their various cabin trunks and heavy suitcases, a tall bearded Indian in a saffron robe and sandals walked up the gangway of the *City of Cairo* carrying his sole piece of luggage — a small leather bag on which was painted the name — Sundar Singh.

PRAYER CHANGES PEOPLE

By prayer we cannot change God's plans, as some people seem to think. But the man who prays is himself changed. The capacities of the soul, which are imperfect in this imperfect life, are daily reaching towards perfection.

A bird sits brooding over her eggs. At first, in the eggs, there is only a kind of liquid without form or shape. But as the mother continues to sit on them, the unformed matter in the eggs becomes changed into the form of the mother. The change is not in the mother but in the eggs. So, when we pray, God is not changed but we are changed into his glorious image and likeness.

Ctenophores or sea gooseberries are so extremely delicate that the splash of a wave would tear them into shreds. Whenever there is even a hint of an approaching storm, they sink deep into the sea, beyond the reach of storm and away from the waves. Just so, when the man of prayer anticipates Satan's attacks and the storm of sin and suffering in the world, at once he dives down into the ocean of God's love where there is eternal peace and calm.

Sadhu Sundar Singh

Chapter

12

For a man born and brought up in North India, the transition to England was like entering a different world — and a grey one. The sky was usually overcast, and in the frequent drizzles of rain black umbrellas added to the dull appearance of the wet streets, from which people hurried to disappear as quickly as possible, sharply closing their front doors behind them. There was none of the leisurely atmosphere of the courtyards and markets of the east, where neighbours had plenty of time to chat and argue, and no one was dominated by the clock. In England everyone seemed silently engrossed with his own affairs, and usually in a hurry. The 1914—1918 War was over and the Peace Treaty had been signed, but the war had left its sombre legacy of bereaved families, still conscious of the loss of the million men who had died in the battlefields.

There was something else that was lacking, too, from Sundar's point of view. In India there was an awareness of spiritual things, a groping for that which would bring peace to the soul. In England he sensed a

155

preoccupation with what would bring material satisfaction, a satisfaction that ignored the deeper needs of the human spirit. He had been in the country less than a month when he was asked what he thought of English Christianity and English life generally. The question was put to him at table, placing him in the awkward position of appearing discourteous to his hosts, and he wisely replied that he had not been in the country long enough to be qualified to pass an opinion. It had struck him, though, that too little was made of religion. He thought that more time should be given to being quiet and just meditating on the word of God. Without prayer and reflection spiritual things could not be understood. He spoke quite spontaneously, and a little hush fell at the table. His brief comment had made a deeper impression than many sermons, for it was obvious to everyone that he knew what he was talking about.

Sundar had made very few arrangements for his stay in England. In one way this was a deliberate policy, for his own faith was kept the sharper and more alive when he was consciously looking each day for the guidance of God. However, a missionary friend in India had arranged for him to be met at Liverpool, and from there he was taken first to a well-known Bible teacher, Rendell Harris, then to Selly Oak to live with Quakers, after that to Oxford to stay with the High Anglican community of the Cowley Fathers. He was equally at home with them all, fitting in with all their arrangements quite naturally.

It was while he was in Oxford that he met the man who perhaps more than anyone else was to perpetuate his memory. A. J. Appasamy, who was doing a postgraduate course at the University, had heard about Sundar, not only from his father with whom Sundar had stayed for several weeks in South India, but also from what had been published about him. He was particularly interested in Sundar's mystical experiences, for he had been studying the subject of mysticism for some years, and it was mainly for this reason that he wanted to meet him. There was an immediate rapport between the two young Indians, and Sundar, who made no mystery of what he saw and heard in the invisible realm, was quite ready to answer Appasamy's questions. He agreed, too, to speak at a number of meetings in the University, which Appasamy promptly organised, and which were attended by tutors and clergymen as well as students.

The outcome of the week Sundar spent in Oxford was that Appasamy's tutor, Canon B. H. Streeter, suggested to Sundar that a record of his teaching should be made, and that Appasamy should spend a fortnight or so with him, making notes. It was an arrangement that worked well, for to be accompanied by a fellow countryman who was accustomed to western ways (Appasamy had studied theology in America before coming to Oxford) undoubtedly eased things for Sundar in those early days. They went to Cambridge on leaving Oxford, and then to London where, in addition to the meetings at which he was invited to speak everywhere he went, there were interviews, some with eminent people who wished to meet this sadhu from India about whom they had already heard, and who was attracting so much attention in this country. The Archbishop of Canterbury received him warmly, and merely smiled when Sundar told him that in addition to preaching in Anglican churches he had accepted invitations to speak at Westminster Chapel and the Metropolitan Tabernacle.

'That is quite all right — for *you*,' he said. The young sadhu had been baptised and confirmed in the Anglican Church, but it was recognised that he was

157

not to be confined to it. He knelt devoutly to receive the Archbishop's blessing before he left, tacitly acknowledging his ecclesiastical authority. But it was on this very point that Baron von Hugel, the distinguished Roman Catholic theologian and philosopher expressed his only reservation about Sundar. He pointed out that in spite of the visions and ecstasies experienced by the notable Christian mystics of the past, they had placed themselves under ecclesiastical authority and direction, and he felt Sundar ought to do the same. When Sundar was later questioned about the matter, he replied,

'Concerning my membership in the Church, I must say that I belong to the Body of Christ, the true Church. That cannot be understood as a building of tiles and stones, but as a body of true Christians, living and dead. But I have nothing against anyone becoming a member of an organised Church on earth. In this sense I am a member of the Church of England in India. I don't believe in the Apostolic Succession, but if this belief is a help to people in their spiritual life, then let them believe in it! . . .

'I believe in the Eucharist and in baptism. Every Christian indeed has to obey the commands of the Lord concerning these sacraments, because they are the means of great blessing. Not because the Eucharist becomes the true body of Christ or because there is anything special in water, bread or wine, but because of the obedience towards our Lord. Of course, all this depends on faith.'

Among the many social invitations he received was one from Buckingham Palace. The Queen requested the pleasure of his company to tea and to his distress he saw that at the time appointed he was due to address a congregation of some two thousand people. He took seriously the exhortation to give honour to whom honour is due, and it was with genuine regret that he eventually wrote to explain to Her Majesty why he asked to be excused.

He very rarely referred to this incident, but there was one of a very different nature that he gleefully related again and again. London was often enveloped in thick fogs in those days, and he was standing on a kerb on one occasion, waiting to cross the road, when he was surprised to find that an elderly woman holding a letter in her hand was trying to post it in him. In his long pinkish-coloured robe reaching to the ground, she had mistaken him for a pillar box.

He spent four and a half months in the British Isles with scarcely a break from speaking at a succession of meetings, except for a few days spent in Paris with Appasamy.

'You can now say that you have been in the third heaven, like St Paul,' he said with a grin as they descended from the third floor of the Eiffel Tower. When he was asked what he wanted to see, he said he wanted to see anything connected with the Church generally, especially martyrs for Christ. In the Louvre the picture that attracted him most was that of St Sebastian pierced with arrows. It was, in his view, the best picture in the famous art museum. But even in Paris people got wind of his presence, and two meetings were arranged at which he spoke before he returned to England where he was again caught up in a full and busy programme.

Although the larger meetings naturally attracted more attention, it was at the smaller, informal gatherings that he was most effective. 'I am inclined to feel that it is not the best service we can render to the sadhu if we employ him mainly for big meetings...he is best with small groups or with individuals. I know of a number of definite conversions among people of all ranks of society over here, due to having contact with him,' an English friend of his wrote to America, where Sundar was planning to go next. By this time urgent requests for him to speak were coming in from all quarters, but he had to refuse them. He was conscious of the familiar urge, the call to move on, and it was to America he knew he should go. He arrived in New York at the end of May, and declining the money-making lecture tour that an enterprising firm was eager to organise, accepted the arrangements made for him by Dr F. N. D. Buchman, at that time a lecturer in a theological seminary in Connecticut. At the inaugural meeting held there it was announced that:

'The sadhu is a remarkable and significant person in the Christian world today. He is specially anxious to counteract the influence of the many Swamis and other people who have been over in Europe and America trying to capture certain types of mind for theosophy, Hindu mysticism, etc.'

That Sundar made a deep impression with his Christ-centred awareness of the unseen realm there is no doubt, not only in churches and schools, but at students' conferences and meetings for businessmen. People streamed to hear him, listening eagerly to his experiences and parables, and his reiteration of the importance of knowing God in a personal way, not merely knowing about him. 'What are we aiming at, after all, in studying theology?' one pastor found himself thinking as he sat, surrounded by scholars in gown and hood, watching Sundar and listening to him. 'What are we doing with all our apparatus of scholarship, and what have we achieved by it? Men like this Indian can move nations...But we...?'

Sundar was in America for less than two months,

but in that time he toured from east to west, speaking in New York, Boston, Philadelphia among other places. Some prominent religious personalities who represented modern theology, and who explained away miracles, were surprised and rather alarmed when they saw how students in the exclusive eastern universities readily received his message, with its emphasis on the supernatural.

'I believe entirely in the actual power of Christ, now as in the days of his life on earth, to heal and work what men are pleased to know as "miracles",' he told a reporter in New York, 'I believe not only because of faith, but because of experience.'

A number of articles appeared about him in the press, for he provided journalists with good 'copy', not only by what he said but also by his appearance and manner of life. As he stood beside Silver Bay on Lake George at a students' conference, the rays of the setting sun lighting up the hills beyond, 'it was hard to realise that the lake was not Galilee, the time was not AD 33, and the striking figure not that of the Lord Jesus...' wrote one reporter, while another, in lighter vein, remarked that the sadhu had solved the luggage problem, for all he had was a small leather kit-bag containing his Bible and a spare saffron robe. As for laundering, he did it himself, washing his robe in a hotel bowl and hanging it up to dry on a clothes stand. Thus equipped he was ready for a six months' tour to any part of the world.

He was ready for it in more than practical ways, too. He had not planned to go to Australia, but booked a passage there when he discovered there was no steamer travelling direct from San Francisco to India. His arrival in Sydney was unexpected, but as soon as it was known that he was there he was invited to speak. Seven hundred clergy and Christian workers gathered in the Chapter House of St Andrew's Cathedral to hear him, and later in Pitt Street Church. For both meetings the audiences overflowed and it was the same when he went on to Melbourne and preached in the Cathedral, as well as in some of the larger churches in the city. In Adelaide, too, and in Perth he spoke at meetings that were so full the doors had to be closed half an hour before the time announced for the sadhu to appear on the platform.

'I am having overflow meetings. Very often I have to speak a second time after I have finished speaking at one meeting.' He felt the strain of the unrelieved concentration that was necessary, and said so in a letter to a friend, admitting that on account of the language it was very hard to speak at another meeting immediately. 'But the Holy Spirit enables me to do this for his glory.'

'The Holy Spirit enables me...' To him there was nothing magical about the enabling of the Holy Spirit. It did not absolve him from the hard work involved in mastering the language through which he could communicate to the greatest number of people. On the contrary, it nerved his endeavour to apply his mind to the task. It was while he was in Australia that Rebecca Parker started receiving letters from him written in English instead of Hindustani, and signed 'Your ever loving son, Sundar.'

As in England and America, Sundar's appearance and manner made an indelible impression on those who saw and heard him. At thirty-one years of age he had reached a maturity of manhood, and one wrote of him,

'...a unique figure dressed in his saffron robe and sandals, with a radiant unwrinkled face, full-bearded and a certain calm and majesty of countenance, he

162

seemed to me, as a young Christian, the nearest that I could imagine our Lord looked like.'

This was the impression gained by many of those who saw him in public, but those who saw him in the intimacy of their own homes had close-ups that were even more revealing.

The sudden opening of a door to reveal a little fair-haired girl standing at the sadhu's knees, smiling up into his face as he bent his head down to talk to her...

The little boy who came down to breakfast demanding to know where Jesus was. 'He was here yesterday. I saw him. He played with me...!'

And the hostess who wrote to her son saying,

'It is wonderful having Sundar Singh here; it is unlike anything else that has ever happened. It is indescribable, but it is like having Christ in the house, as near as one can imagine what that would be like!'

'The man who conquered the west'. So was Sundar enthusiastically described by a group of Christians in Madras who were preparing to welcome him back after his eight months' preaching tour in the English-speaking world. Great receptions were being planned for him there and in other places in South India, about which he knew nothing until he reached Colombo. The prospect of being lionised in this way, and being given such a title filled him with dismay. He had once seen a notice in huge letters as he had walked across the campus of one of the universities where he was due to speak, announcing him as 'the world famous sadhu'. Years later he told his friend Riddle, 'When I saw it I was so ashamed that perspiration poured out of me!'

Rather than face the adulation of his admirers he let no one but Vincent David know when he was due to arrive in Bombay, and after telling him about the tour

163

and the impression he had gained of Christianity in the west, he went quietly back to Subathu, leaving Vincent David to pass on to others what he had been told. A few days later a summary of the conversation appeared in *The Christian Patriot* newspaper, commencing,

'Our dearest brother Sadhu Sundar Singh landed in Bombay safe and sound on the 24 September, and told us about his work in England, America and Australia, and his opinion about those places.

'He said many Englishmen of the present day did not believe in the miracles of our Lord Jesus Christ, and when they asked him questions concerning the miracles, the sadhu answered them and added that he saw a miracle wrought amongst them because, in spite of the English people being so materialistic, there were many spiritual people among them...

'There is a good deal of Christianity in America, but that is not enough...Our Lord's words, "Come unto me, all ye that labour and are heavy laden, and I will give you rest," are true as regards the east, but the sadhu thinks that as for America our Lord would say, "Come unto me, all ye that labour and are heavy gold-laden and I will give you rest."

'Still, God has his own witnesses in the west and all over the world. Sometimes young Indians say that they do not want missionaries from such places, but that is a mistake. The sadhu thinks that the missionaries from the west who come to India keep alive the churches at home, and if the west did not send us missionaries, very soon their churches would become dead like the Dead Sea. So we should welcome the missionaries for the sake of keeping Christianity alive in the west. The sadhu's experience is that no country or nation in this world is Christian. It is individuals who are Christians — individuals who live and are in touch with Jesus Christ...' The long article concluded with words of Sundar himself, in which he was reported as having said,

'I have not finished my tour in Europe. God willing, after visiting Tibet next year, if God opens the way I might go to the places where people so earnestly invited me; namely, Sweden, Switzerland, and other European countries.'

Eighteen months later he was on his way there, clad as always in his saffron robe and only sandals on his bare feet. By this time the book written by Canon Streeter and Appasamy, *The Sadhu* had been published, and along with Rebecca Parker's book was being translated into some of the European languages. Great interest in this unusual figure from the east was being aroused, not only among eminent religionists and theologians.

On his way to Europe he was granted the desire of his heart in visiting Palestine, walking through the streets of Jerusalem, by the Lake of Galilee, visiting Bethlehem, Nazareth, the Jordan...His host was Sir William Willcocks, who had built the Aswan Dam in Egypt. In Sweden he was the guest of Prince Bernadotte, brother of the King. In Denmark the Dowager Empress of Russia invited him to her castle. And as in the case of his Master, 'the common people heard him gladly.'

But among the religionists and theologians there was a different spirit. Convictions and feelings began to deepen, and in the violent controversy that broke out after his five months preaching tour in Europe, some proved themselves his ardent and loyal supporters while others became his violent and vehement critics and accusers.

USING THINGS ARIGHT

There is no evil or harm in using any of God's created things, provided that we do it with thankfulness and with a proper sense of their value. Danger lies in giving the Creator's places in our heart to the creature. We should give to the Creator the Creator's place, and to the creature the creature's. We can neither live without water, nor live in the water. We must drink, but not sink. If we do not drink we shall die of thirst; if we sink we shall die of drowning. So we must use the things of the world in such a way that, while they sustain our bodies, they do not become too strong for us and choke the vital breath of our lives, which is prayer.

With and Without Christ

13

When Sundar disembarked at Marseilles at six o'clock one Sunday morning in February 1922, he was informed that he was booked to speak in the Swiss church in the morning and the French Reformed Church in the evening. Then he was to board the express to Geneva, and after travelling all night, change trains, to arrive in Lausanne where he would be met by a few of those who were planning his itinerary in Switzerland.

Not surprisingly, when he got off the train at this destination, he looked slightly dazed, and beyond a courteous bow of the head and a smile as he was introduced, he made no effort to communicate with his escort on the way up to a spacious chalet in the mountains. He wanted to be quiet before meeting the committee with their plan of campaign for the weeks he was to spend in their country. They were well prepared. A map was spread out on the table before him, and the various towns and cities where he was booked to speak pointed out. He had a good memory, and made a swift but accurate mental note of the times and places. He saw that it was a very full programme, but agreed to it all, making only one stipulation.

'Don't make me speak more than once a day, except on Sunday,' he said. 'It is not like giving a lesson in school. That can become a routine affair, and carry no blessing.' To him, preaching was not something that could be produced automatically. Every time he knew he was to speak he spent a long time in prayer, seeking the right message, memorising what he wanted to say, for he never made notes from which to read. And he knew that in Europe the language problem would be increased, for he understood neither French nor German. He must think in Hindustani, speak in English, and rely on his interpreters to convey his message in whichever language was required.

'I am very tired,' he admitted when, after a few weeks in Europe, someone enquired how he was feeling. A string of social engagements and private interviews day after day, had added to the strain. And on another occasion, in the course of a conversation with a German pastor, he referred to the heaviness of the atmosphere.

'Yes, the climatic conditions here are very different from India,' the pastor observed.

Sundar shook his head. 'I'm not referring to the physical atmosphere,' he said. 'In India one feels everywhere, even through the idols and the temples, the pilgrims and the penitents, there is a desire for higher things. Here...' he paused for a moment, then went on,

'Here everything points to armed force, great power and material things. It is the power from below that makes me sad.' There were times when he spoke out publicly, especially towards the end of his tour, what he felt about Europe,

'In non-Christian countries men worship idols

168

made with hands; in the so-called Christian countries I find a worse kind of heathenism — men worship themselves. When you see Christ in his glory, then you will grieve that you did not believe in him as your God. But then it will be too late. You have allowed yourselves to be led astray by unbelievers — by intellectual men who said you should not believe in his divinity. Repentance then will be too late. Perhaps in that day you will hear it said, "A man came to you from a heathen land; he bore witness to me as the living Christ because he had experienced my power and my glory, and yet you would not believe..." '

From Switzerland and Germany he went to Sweden, Norway and Denmark, and finally to Holland. Everywhere he went meetings were organised at which he was the speaker, and people flocked to hear him. As someone said of him,

'He draws souls like a magnet.'

It was noticeable that although the main points of his sermons were usually the same, with their emphasis on the importance of prayer and a personal relationship with Jesus Christ, he spoke from a different text, with different arguments and illustrations, each time. And as the weeks passed, he referred less and less to his own miraculous deliverances and visions, drawing more on parables from nature to make his point. He realised the danger of people trying to imitate him, or seeking the same sort of spiritual experiences. As for the visions about which Canon Streeter and Appasamy had written so much in their book, he made it plain to people who asked him about them that he himself gave weight to them only so far as they were in harmony with what was in the Bible.

With many social engagements pressed into his programme, the mental and emotional strain of living constantly in the public eye was as great in its way as the physical hardships endured in the rugged, icy regions of Tibet. Perhaps greater. By the time his tour was over and he made his way back to India, he was exhausted in mind and body. It was several weeks before he was restored to his normal vigour and from that time ill health began to dog him. But he had made an impact on the Christianity of the western world that was unforgettable.

'My dearest Mother,' wrote Sundar to Rebecca Parker from Simla. The letter was dated 1 June 1924. 'I arrived here yesterday...owing to my weak lungs I could not cross the high mountains on my way to Tibet, so I had to return without going there.' There was another reason why he could not get there — a political reason. 'I am sorry to say that our school in Tibet had to be closed owing to opposition from the officials. A member of the British Buddhist Mission, after seeing the school, wrote an article in *The Statesman* asking why they, as Buddhists, were not allowed to go to Tibet, but Christians are allowed to have a school there. When the officials read that article, they ordered the school to be closed.' Then he continued, 'Still, the Lord is doing his work in another way. Now I will continue to work in the Himalayan states where the gospel has not been preached, and in the winter I will attend several conferences and conventions.'

Two years had passed since his return from Europe, and a number of changes had taken place in his life during that time. For one thing, he at last had a home of his own. His father had died, leaving him half his entire estate, and while Sundar had handed over the property to his brother, he had kept the money. With it he had bought an old mission house in Subathu. He retained a room for himself; the rest of the house was occupied by Dr V. W. Peoples, a medical man connected with the leprosy work, and his family.

To this place Sundar could always return. His home was the room in which there were photographs of his friends, and pictures of Christ in Gethsemane, Christ preaching the sermon on the mount, and also the popular picture of Christ sitting with the children of five different races around him, revealing Sundar's own love for children.

Here he dealt with the volume of letters that came to him from all parts of the world, many of them letters urging him to return, inviting him to speak at conventions or conduct missions. Sometimes several such invitations would arrive in one day, and laughingly he said to his friends,

'You'd better make soup of me, and let everyone have a spoonful!' But letters from abroad, from America, Europe, England, Australia, all received the same reply. He would not be leaving India again.

It was during those two years that he had become the target for virulent criticism and accusation on the part of religionists who openly opposed him. A series of articles appeared in one Roman Catholic publication denouncing him as an impostor. He had never been to Tibet. The story of his imprisonment in a well of dead men's rotting corpses was a downright lie. He himself had sent off the telegram announcing his death at the time of his 'fast', thus attracting attention to himself. And so on. A Protestant pastor in Switzerland attacked him from another angle in a book which set out to prove that the sadhu was self-deceived, that the miraculous experiences about which he spoke were merely the figments of his own imagination.

Sundar himself was not unduly worried by these attacks, although he had been quite perturbed by something that had happened while he was on one of his journeys up the passes towards Tibet. On his return he had learned that once again a rumour had been spread that he was dead. It had apparently started with a Bombay paper reporting that it was rumoured that the sadhu, Sundar Singh, was no longer alive. This was taken up by various papers in India and Europe, and eventually ended up in *The Daily News* in England, which had been informed 'on good authority' that Buddhist fanatics in Tibet had murdered the Indian Christian mystic and saint, Sadhu Sundar Singh.

'My dearest Mother,' he had written to Rebecca Parker after sending her a telegram reassuring her that he was alive and well. 'I am surprised to see how this false rumour is spreading everywhere. I can't understand how or where it started. I think an enemy must be responsible for this...' While those who opposed him were not slow to imply that once again he had instigated the whole thing, those who knew him best all supported him. That in the ardour of his youth he had exaggerated or misinterpreted some of his experiences they did not deny. His assertion that he had fasted for forty days when all the evidence went to prove it was only half that time was a case in point. Sundar had always been more concerned with the realities of the unseen world than with the facts and figures of the world that can be seen. But it had never been with intent to deceive. Dr Fife and Bishop Lefroy who had known him from his boyhood, Dr Wherry and the Rev. T. E. Riddle who had been closely associated with him since his early days as a sadhu, were all prepared to vouch for his sincerity.

Among those who took up the cudgels on his behalf without any personal knowledge of him was an eminent German professor who went to endless trouble to investigate the accusations made against him. In all,

Professor F. Heiler wrote three books about Sadhu Sundar Singh, in one of them placing him in the succession of such Christian mystics as St Francis of Assisi, St Augustine, St Thomas Aquinas, St Catherine of Genoa, and others.

Archbishop Soderholm of Uppsala was another European who vehemently defended him in writing. His prophecy that the controversy, which lasted for years through a dark chapter in church history, could not but serve God's Kingdom, proved true. Interest in the sadhu and his teaching was kept alive and stimulated by it, so that when his own books came off the press there was an instant and wide demand for them.

For Sundar had started to write. His first book, produced in 1921, took the form of a conversation between a disciple and his Master, with questions being asked and answered. He did not claim that it was without fault, for as he wrote, rather diffidently, in the foreword,

'There is nothing so perfect in the world as to be quite above objection and criticism. The very sun which gives us light and warmth is not free from spots, yet notwithstanding these defects it does not desist from its regular duty. It behoves us in like manner to carry on to the best of our ability what has been entrusted to us, and strive constantly to make our lives fruitful.

'When the truths set forth in this book were revealed to me by the Master they deeply affected my life, and some of them have been used by me in my sermons and addresses in Europe, America, Australia and Asia. At the request of many friends I have now gathered them together in this little book, and though it is possible that there are defects in setting them forth, I am sure that those who read them with prayer

173

and an unprejudiced mind, will benefit from them as I have.'

In the years that followed he wrote five more. If he could not preach verbally he would preach on paper. For his health was failing. Not only were his lungs weak, but he started to have heart attacks. 'You've crushed your heart with overwork,' his doctor told him, but Sundar told his friends that it had been his desire to sacrifice his youth in his Master's service, and he was glad that his prayer had been granted. With his instinct for parables he said,

'It is better to burn quickly and melt many souls than to burn slowly and melt none.'

Then his eyesight was affected. An operation performed by an Indian eye specialist was successful, but the time came when he always needed to wear dark glasses. The enforced physical inactivity imposed by pain and ill health meant that he spent even more time in prayer and meditation, while the periods of ecstasy continued from which he always emerged refreshed and renewed, with a light on his face which quietened and slightly awed those who saw him. One young student who met him briefly in Calcutta early in 1929 wrote,

'It is said that when Dante passed through the streets of Florence people would draw back and whisper to one another, "That man has been in Hell." Few who have seen the strange Indian mystic who passed through Calcutta the other day and whose name has become so familiar to the world during the last decade, could withhold from him the claim he makes, that he has seen heaven...For upon the face of that person there is a look one seldom sees anywhere else. It is the look of one whose eyes have gazed upon the unseen, whose ears have heard things others do not hear — to whom the beating of angels' wings is as real as the street cries outside.'

Sundar had a voluminous correspondence. Letters arrived every day from abroad as well as places in India, and he replied, even if sometimes quite briefly, to all the letters he received. He was business-like in this, as well as in his financial affairs. He had put the bulk of the money left him by his father into a trust, into which he also paid all the royalties that came in from his books. In this way he was able to help support evangelists connected with the indigenous National Missionary Society of India in Madras, and provide a home for some boys he was seeing through school. One missionary who had travelled for several days in order to meet him found him sitting on the doorstep of his house, buying eggs.

'It's Christmas, you know!' he said as though in explanation of what looked like extravagance. And later, at the table, as the boys stirred sugar into his tea, with an apologetic smile,

'They know I have a weakness for sweet things.' Those who visited him found him a very natural and easy host.

In spite of the physical infirmities that kept him so often at home, the urge to preach never left him, and most months found him taking journeys, sometimes involving two or three days in the train, to speak at conferences and missions in various parts of India. And always there was that indefinable call of the Himalayas range, and the land beyond it — Tibet.

'I want to go once more to Tibet,' he wrote to his friend Riddle, and in April, 1927 he set off with some Tibetan traders, making towards the Niti Pass. He had only travelled some forty miles, however, when he had a severe haemorrhage and was carried back to the railway only half-conscious. He was ill for some time, and had to give up the idea of going to Tibet that year. During the following months he made several tours in India, and applied his mind very diligently to the book he was writing. It was a tedious task for him. 'I have no taste for writing!' he often remarked, but the sense of compulsion to complete the book *With and Without Christ* was strong. With the help of Riddle he completed the English translation in August 1928.

It was the last book he ever wrote.

Preaching tours in India continued, but writing to Rebecca Parker at Christmas he told her he was hoping to start for Tibet in March or April. Then he went to see Riddle, who was one of the trustees of his will. He wanted to ensure that everything was in order, for he always went up those passes into Tibet with the consciousness that he might never return. He spoke about his longing to go to Rasar, to the east of Lake Mansarowar, where he heard there were now some Christians. He became very excited as he spoke, and then there was a pause in the conversation and Riddle saw, to his surprise, that Sundar was trembling.

What was the matter? That trembling was the trembling of fear, something he had never seen in Sundar before. It could not be the fear of death — he faced the possibility of death every time he went to Tibet. Death! Sundar welcomed it. To him it would be the door through which he would pass to be forever in that bright realm which he visited in his ecstasies, returning to the world reluctantly, as to a prison. No, he was not afraid of death. What had caused that sudden, involuntary fit of trembling had been the memory of the horror of the darkness he had experienced in the well at Rasar, into which he had been flung years before...What if it should happen again...?

The spasm passed, and Sundar was himself

176

again — but it had revealed something of what it meant to him when he told his friends he was leaving for Tibet 'fully aware of the dangers and difficulties of the journey.' To which he added the words, 'But I must do my best to do my duty.'

April 1929 dawned. He was in touch with some Tibetan traders who undertook to let him know when they would be setting out for Tibet, by way of the Niti Pass. Everything was in readiness for when the message came, so when, in the middle of the month, he was told to come immediately to join the party at Rishikesh on the Ganges, all he had to do was to write two or three short letters, and set off. One letter was to Riddle. In it he quoted Acts 20:24, and continued,

'I wanted to come to see you before leaving for Tibet, but I have received a letter from a trader to meet him at once on our way to Tibet. The route will be the same as that I told you about last year. I hope to be back with one or two Tibetan Christians by the end of June. If anything happens I will send down Thapa to meet you, but if you do not hear anything about me, or from me, then please come to Subathu in July to see to all my things in the house here.'

Then he looked at the little photograph of Rebecca Parker on his desk, and drew a sheet of paper towards him to write to her. The letter was dated 18 April 1929.

'My dearest Mother. I am leaving today for Tibet. Please don't be anxious for me. God's will may be done. I know that you will be praying for me, for which I thank you from the bottom of my heart. I, too, will continue to pray for you.

'I will let you know at once if the Lord brings me back safely. Otherwise Mr Riddle will give you information, and we shall meet again at Jesus' blessed feet forever.

'I know the dangers and difficulties of this journey, but must obey him.'

Again he wrote 'Acts 20:24.' Then he concluded his letter with the words,

'Now with much love to both of you I close this letter. May God bless you still more abundantly, Amen,

'Your loving son, Sundar.'

He glanced through it, was just about to put it in the envelope, then scribbled a post-script at the top. 'P.S. I hope to be back here in June.'

There was one more thing to be done. He went along the ridge, with its views of the plains on one side and the pine-forested hills leading to the snow-capped range of the Himalayas on the other, to the home of the superintendent of the asylum for leprosy patients. He went to say goodbye, to explain the route he planned to take, and to say that he expected to be back in Subathu before the end of June.

'I'll be out of reach of the post, of course,' he went on. 'I'll be very grateful if you will receive my correspondence, and reply to any letters that need answering immediately. Thank you very much...Good-bye...' And so the saffron-robed figure passed down the ridge and out of sight, for the last time. Twenty years had passed since, as a young man of nineteen, he had first set his face towards that snow-capped range and the land that lay beyond. He walked more slowly now, and dark glasses shielded his weak eyes from the glare of the sun, but again he was heading for Tibet. The verse he had referred to in both of his letters, Acts 20:24, applied to him now, and he knew it.

'I consider my life worth nothing to me, if only I may finish the race and complete the task the Lord Jesus has given me — the task of testifying to the gospel of God's grace.' And those among whom he had gone preaching that gospel, saw him again no more.

For, like Enoch, Sundar walked with God. And he was not. For God took him.

WHAT HAPPENS AT DEATH?

One day when I was praying alone, I suddenly found myself surrounded by a great concourse of spirit beings, or I might say that as soon as my spiritual eyes were opened I found myself bowed in the presence of a considerable company of saints and angels. At first I was somewhat abashed, when I saw their bright and glorious state and compared with them my own inferior quality. But I was at once put at ease by their real sympathy and love-inspired friendliness. I had already had the experience of the peace of the presence of God in my life, but the fellowship of these saints added a new and wonderful joy to me...

That time is not far distant when my readers will pass over into the spiritual world, and see these things with their own eyes. But before we leave this world for ever to go to our eternal home, we must with the support of God's grace, and in the spirit of prayer, carry out with faithfulness our appointed work. Thus shall we fulfil the purpose of our lives, and enter, without any shade of regret, into the eternal joy of the kingdom of our Heavenly Father.

The Spiritual World

EPILOGUE

The mystery of the disappearance of Sadhu Sundar Singh after leaving Subathu on 18 April 1929 has never been solved. The route he was to have taken was one he had often travelled before, having returned from a visit to Rishikesh in the Ganges Valley on New Year's Day, 1929. He had written to Rev. Thomas Riddle about it, telling him, 'I have had very useful conversations with the Secret Sanyasi Mission's leaders there.' From Rishikesh, where he was to have joined the Tibetan traders, he had planned to go with them along the Pilgrim Line, mingling with thousands of Hindu pilgrims making their way to one of the sources of the Ganges. Then, as travelling became increasingly perilous, along narrow paths on steep mountainsides, across swiftly flowing rivers, in bitingly cold weather, and so to the Niti Pass and the border into Tibet.

None of his friends expected to hear from him for at least six weeks. He had told them he expected to return some time in June, and so it was not until about the middle of that month that they began to get anxious. By July they knew that something must have happened to him, or he would certainly have written or sent them a message. So his friend Riddle, along with another missionary, set out to travel the route he was to have taken, going two hundred and twenty miles into the main range of the Himalayas, trying to get news of him. They were away for twenty-eight hazardous and adventurous days, but returned without having heard anything of him. No one who knew him along that route had seen him. The road he would have travelled along the Pilgrim Line passed within fifty yards of the home of an old Christian preacher, and Sundar, who loved his friends, would not have failed to call in and see him if he had got so far. And even if he had gone beyond, through the Bhotia tribal villages, he could easily have been traced, for not many travelled that way, and he would undoubtedly have been noted and remembered. No one had seen him, or heard anything of him.

Reports of his disappearance appeared in newspapers all over the world, and wild speculations as to what had happened to him ranged from murder, to his having retreated to a remote cave to spend the rest of his life in solitary prayer like the Maharishi of Kailash. He might have had a heart attack, or slipped off a narrow mountain path. The most likely explanation of what happened, and the view taken by Mr Riddle, is that he died in the cholera epidemic that swept away many of the pilgrims along the Ganges Valley at that time, whose bodies were thrown into the river, no record concerning them being possible.

By whatever means God took his servant home, he evidently did not intend it to be known. There is nothing in the death he died to distract attention from the outstanding influence of the life he lived. He founded no work, established no order, was of no political significance, yet his name is still remembered, and books about him continue to be written sixty and more years after his disappearance. It was not only his single-minded, unremitting work as a preacher that stirred the sluggard and fired the ardent. There was something else. The tall, bearded, barefooted man in the saffron robe of an Indian sadhu, Sundar Singh brought with him an indefinable sense of the Eternal. It was not only his physical appearance that made people murmur, 'He reminds me of Jesus Christ.' It was the quality of his personality. And behind that lay the outstanding experience that transformed his life — a life which continues to be both an inspiration and a challenge.

It is a challenge because year after year he turned away from the crowds that thronged to hear him preach, to take his solitary journey through the Himalayan foothills into the closed land of Tibet. His purpose was to do his part in completing the Church's unfinished task of proclaiming the gospel of God's grace in all the world, as a witness to all nations. It is an inspiration because, as a meteor flashing across the sky lifts man's eyes from earth to the heavens, so those who met him in the workaday world became aware that there is another realm — a heavenly realm, peopled with angels and saints, where Jesus Christ the Lord reigns. And this is Reality. 'So we fix our eyes, not on what is seen, but on what is unseen. For what is seen is temporary, but what is unseen is eternal.'